[OURS] HYPERLOCALIZATION OF ARCHITECTURE

Published by eVolo Press

6363 Wilshire Boulevard, Suite 311

Los Angeles, California 90048

Visit our website at www.evolo.us

Front cover image RMIT Design Hub by Sean Godsell Architects

Front cover design and photo © Andrew Michler

Author photograph Laura Cofrin

Design Andrew Michler, Carlo Aiello

Design assistance red letter creative

Copy editing Brigette Brown, Evelyn Ashcroft

All photos © Andrew Michler unless otherwise noted

All drawings and diagrams © of the Architects

Every reasonable attempt has been made to identify owners of copyrights. Errors or omissions will be corrected in subsequent editions or online.

ISBN: 978-1938740084 (hardback)

First Edition

Printed in China

Printed on paper made from post consumer recycled content

HYPERLOCALIZATION

OF

ARCHITECTURE

CONTEMPORARY SUSTAINABLE ARCHETYPES

ANDREW MICHLER

Generosity is the virtue that produces peace

-Sutra of the Recollection of the Noble Three Jewels

Craig Michler

LIVING INDEX

SOL Grotto by Rael San Frantello Architects

To provide further resources a companion website provides updated multimedia, maps, photos of the architects, sections and floor plans, and unpublished documentation of projects.

Visit www.hyperlocalarch.com

To use the QR code accompanying each project download a QR Reader app for your tablet or smart phone. Each code goes directly to the project's web-page.

Researchers

Rachel Ashton

Sam Hartley

Dr. Katharine Leigh

Erin Nuckols

Tara Seegers

Aaron Wagner

Research assistance provided by the
Institute for the Built Environment
Colorado State University
Fort Collins, Colorado
www.ibe.colostate.edu

Kickstarter Backers

Sandra Antongiorgi

Evelyn Ashcroft

Dottie Barnett

Colin Berriman

Wendy Bredehoft

Yshmael Cabana

Loretta Cummings

Aren Jensen

David Thompson

Nathan Staas

Thank you

Carlo Aiello

Benjamin Albertson

Lloyd Alter

Anthony and Donna Barnett

Lauren Burke

Loretta Cummings

Jenifer Davey

Anthony Denzer

Brian Dunbar

Camellia El-Antably in memory of Samir El-Antably

Mike Eliason

Clark Erwin

Jill Fehrenbacher and the Inhabitat team

William Galloway

Yumi Goto

Nic Granleese

Lex Hundsdorfer

Brian Hull

Trine Jeppesen

Jacqueline Kruithof

Craig Michler

in memory of Micheal T. Murphy

A special thank you to the architects who opened their studios, projects, and homes. The quality of your honest inquiry into the meaning of design lays the path for how we shall live in a greater harmony with the Earth and each other.

To my wife Jennie, who understands beauty better than anyone I have ever met.

Lloyd Alter has practiced as an architect, has been a real estate developer, and prefab housing entrepreneur. He teaches sustainable design at Ryerson University in Toronto and writes for the Guardian, Corporate Knights Magazine, Azure, and is editor of TreeHugger.com.

The Guggenheim Museum in Bilbao is a wonderful pile. It revolutionized how we think of the role of buildings in our cities; it was the original demonstration of what is now known as the "Bilbao effect" where a building is powerful enough that it revitalizes a whole community. However, if you hold a photo of it up beside a photo of the Walt Disney concert hall in Los Angeles, I challenge you to tell which one is which. They are both aliens, dropped into a milieu where they stand out like sore thumbs, as they were meant to. The same can be said for many of the so-called "starchitect"- designed buildings from Rem to Zaha. The same is true for your typical glass office building or subdivision house; they could be anywhere. They are devoid of place. But place matters.

Christopher Alexander wrote: *This is a fundamental view of the world. It says that when you build a thing you cannot merely build that thing in isolation, but must repair the world around it, and within it, so that the larger world at that one place becomes more coherent, and more whole; and the thing which you make takes its place in the web of nature, as you make it.*

This is why Andrew Michler's concept of hyperlocalization is so fascinating and valuable. Because every building he shows is not only a product of its climate and its environment, but of its history, its culture, a reflection of the personalities of the people who built it and surround it. So Passivhaus is so very German, engineering-driven and mathematical, built like a Mercedes. So building in Cascadia is so woody and hippie. So houses in Japan are so tiny and betray a totally different understanding of privacy and permanence. So Danes like to move.

There is another aspect beside the respect for culture that comes from thinking hyperlocally: respect for climate. Years ago Barbara Flanagan wrote in ID Magazine in a discussion of the effects of air conditioning: "What happens when humans treat themselves like dairy products chilled behind glass? Civilization declines. The proof is in Barcelona. Spend five glorious weeks in its barely mitigated heat, as I did last summer, then return home and refrigerate yourself in the relentless mono-temperature now anesthetizing the continent. Conclusion? A/C is the killing frost sure to wilt the last fragile shoots of American culture."

In a hyperlocalized world, people and buildings adapt to climate. They minimize the use of expensive technologies and work with wind, shading, natural, tried and true methods that are resilient and flexible. If they live in Barcelona they go out and eat dinner late at night. If they live in Tokyo, the streets are their living rooms.

Having a mono-temperature leads to a mono-culture where people move from air conditioned homes to cars to offices and never go outside. Recently I watched an advertisement for a new smart thermostat from Honeywell that followed your phone. It showed a car driving into the suburbs and the GPS on the phone telling the house to crank up the AC so that he can drive straight into the garage and never step outside. These new smart technologies are the antithesis of hyperlocalization, designed to make living in a suburb of Shanghai indistinguishable from Silicon Valley or for that matter, Mars. Technology is attempting to make location and local culture irrelevant.

For all the wonders of this high tech interconnected Internet of Things world, it is dependent on a vast infrastructure of dependable electricity, water and internet connections, which we cannot take for granted anymore. It depends on reliable food supplies and transportation infrastructure that are under incredible pressure. It's based on engineering principles where everybody expects the temperature to be 68 degrees year round, the power and water to run and the thermostat will talk to the fridge and make sure you are comfy and fed. When the electricity fails, the glass towers being built everywhere in the world can become uninhabitable in a matter of hours.

Hyperlocalization ensures resilience. It's based on the history of how people have built in the past, the understanding of how to adapt to climate. The knowledge of how to maintain and repair simpler systems. But most importantly it is based on a deep comprehension of culture, of how people lived and flourished in a particular place. That is something that has been lost in the last few decades. Hyperlocalization is a demonstration that in fact we can learn the lessons from the past and use them as templates for the future.

Andrew Michler and I have danced together around the blogosphere for years. The popular architectural blog world is full of tiny houses and shipping containers and wonderful but imaginary towers, all lovingly pinned and facebooked and tumblred and houzzed and slideshowed. Andrew's work popped out as different; it's clear that he knows something about actually building things. His writing reflects his experience and knowledge. And more.

F. Scott Fitzgerald wrote that "The test of a first rate intelligence is the ability to hold two opposed ideas in the mind at the same time, and still retain the ability to function." Andrew has demonstrated that as well. There are two schools of thought in green building: 1) that reducing energy consumption trumps everything (hence the endless cubic yards of toxic fossil fueled plastic foam insulation in most Passive Houses) 2) that we should build with healthy, non-toxic materials with low embodied energy. Andrew took these two opposed ideas and built the first off-grid and foam free Passive House in the United States. This was no small challenge.

He also took on the challenge of producing a book that is more than just a printed blog, a collection of pretty pictures of buildings. He has traveled widely and chosen carefully, placing them in their context, climate and culture, something that too many architects forget these days. They have much to learn from Andrew and this book; I certainly did.

There are few secrets in architecture. Because it is such a public practice we have to live with both its triumphs and errors that are extracted often only after the building has been well seasoned. A majority of buildings have failed on the most basic level of interacting with the place and people they aspire to serve. A swift walk down many modern city centers will reveal large swaths of concrete, glass, and marble, but very little human-scaled spaces for people to activate. From the observation of how a building operates, it is a humbling experience for the practitioners in the world's largest industry to have to admit that what has happened for the past 70 years has been marked by an extraordinary mistake. The fact that a modern skyscraper will typically use more energy per square meter than a century-old brick mid-rise is sobering. It makes sense when you compare the capacity to control heat with a glass skin to a thick masonry wall, or an artificially lit deep interior to a shallow floor plate with a light well on one side and street on the other. It demonstrates that our indicators of progress in buildings have been divorced from basic consumption. The principle of modern design was severed from the realities of a building as an environmental intervention by relying on technology to overcome conditions rather than adapt to them. Buildings that were more mindful of resources we began to label "green." In a way it was a tepid acknowledgment that we were designing them erroneously this entire time. Architecture failed on a most basic level by not using energy, water, light, and space with wisdom and care, causing great harm to the natural environment while making a big fuss about how it would improve the human condition.

In a city like Melbourne, the many high-rises are remote even though they dominate the city center. They stand aloof to the reality of the human experience on the sidewalks. But something is happing there. The life of the city is squeezed into the laneways originally intended to service these buildings and their Victorian predecessors. In a compelling turnaround, these perfunctory spaces were reclaimed by entrepreneurs and artists in the 2000s and transformed into the soul of the city's gridiron. Originally designed just wide enough for horse carriages to deliver goods and remove trash, the previously overlooked narrow alleys have developed organically. They are now invigorated places to meet friends at a sidewalk café or bar, or experiment with street art or a new business venture. Around any corner you could just as easily find yourself in a kaleidoscope of graffiti or the latest trendy watering hole.

Even more unique is how Melbourne is strewn with provocative and refined buildings of all sizes, which advance a contemporary approach to how architecture can respond to and redefine conditions. Perhaps it is Melbourne's remoteness and embrace of anything new, or a wariness of the heavy Victorian mannerism, and then all the -isms that have followed, or something more goading, but the city is charting its own distinct course. While still just a fraction of the overall construction, there is an extraordinary presence of building projects that boldly anticipate the future of architecture. They are aesthetically authentic; what first may seem obtuse or bewildering is based on sound principles of performance, use, and location. These buildings, big or small, formal or outrageous, all speak a common language of a kinetic or animated engagement with their environment.

This century has witnessed a sea change in what architecture can be. It is as though a reset button has been pressed. Ornamentation was abandoned after the first couple of decades of the 20th century for a modernist movement emulating the perfunctory aesthetic of the machine. The product of architecture was to vastly improve our living condition at scale, and it did for a time. We built relentlessly to a new paradigm where design was universal and fungible. We were given the gift of a clean slate where the past was severed by curtains of suspended glass, and in the background was complex machinery to keep it comfortable and well lit. It was assumed that technology in itself was our salvation. Then came Postmodernism, which was largely a nostalgic sidetrack. Now, in the early part of this century the ubiquitous and globalized modernist archetype is being replaced with an architecture expressing a much larger set of values. The architecture community is still grappling for its identity and terminology. There is a veracious appetite for ideas and the use of powerful design tools and sophisticated engineering to metabolize an entire spectrum of building typologies. It can be argued that we have entered a renaissance of architectural prototyping.

There is an understandable confusion about how to assess these new formulations in terms of environmental and cultural value for the generations they will serve. A certain sector of the profession has made the individual architect the focus. This is not surprising given the great effort put into the branding of personalities, the drive of commissions, the covet of the instant landmark, and the serving of the endless appetite of the media and public. This dynamic has been with us for some time, but has become a phenomenon unto itself, starting in 1997 with the Guggenheim Museum erected in an isolated Spanish mid-sized working-class city. This building is now often referenced but bears repeating.

Frank Gehry ushered in a new design culture of stand-alone bravado, which has helped turn our collective impression of a building into something where shelter making is a secondary concern. The catalyst is new parametric design tools which are the logical extension of a modernist fixation with technology. What changed is that the article of the building's design is itself removed from any context both within and outside. The Guggenheim Bilbao's relationship with its surroundings is incongruous and so it cannot, by design, respond to those conditions. It is an exercise in form making for spectacle, one great ornament with echoes of the pre-modernist era's values. It is less Le Corbusier's "a machine for living," it is a building about only itself.

In 2003, Edward Mazria presented powerful research which indicated that buildings make up about 48% of human-caused carbon emissions. Some in the industry had already been well-aware of the situation for decades, and had voiced their concern about the extraordinary amount of energy and other resources buildings consume. Astonishingly, the environmental impact was simply seen in the mainstream design profession as inconsequential. The distraction of tastes, real estate markets, and value engineering swamped most efforts at progressing the knowledge and implementation of the performance of a building. By the 2000s the recalcitrant industry finally responded but has to relearn the basics first. What exactly defines a green material? How does a building skin lose or gain heat, and how can a building use sunlight properly? How can a smaller building do more work, and where should it be located? What does it mean to design for a climate, and is the solution a question of technology?

Historically we have been branding the idea of environmentally oriented design in terms of aspirations. Presently the term "green" has gone out of fashion as a result of its vagueness and "sustainable" is losing its capacity to capture the imagination. Now new ways of looking at environmental building are being broadcast as "zero net energy," "regenerative," and "resilient."

Technical and aesthetic observations are where most dialog occurs, but the formulation of much broader and deeper inquiries is emerging. As William McDonough often pointedly tells us, nothing is really sustainable. Either it is good and beneficial, or less bad by merely slowing the process of degradation of the environment. A good design creates habitat and abundance, is part of a circular economy, and improves connections, both human and natural. A less bad design reduces the use of raw materials, it requires less pollution to operate, it creates less harm to the inhabitants.

A few of the projects in this book are considered the most environmentally forward thinking in the world, but by themselves they may just edge past the less bad side of this spectrum. What is important is that they provide us with a point of purchase so we can progress in the inquiry of manifesting environmental values in the tissue of design. The conversations with the architects make clear that they are articulating very specific and pragmatic design solutions to deeper concerns than are typically addressed in the design profession. These architects do not dwell on visions of utopia, which is the modernist siren, or dream commissions, which have come to define starchitecture, nor is there much rumination on the past except what we can learn from it. They cultivate a design culture that expresses the potential of environmental design for many different situations. This book starts with place as the pivot of inquiry in all of its complexity, and explores design narratives that best respond to those circumstances. Rather than using the framework of aspirational thinking, the process of using place as catalyst takes the vagaries of concepts and plants them into immediate and highly functional forms. Aspiration architecture, that which responds to the important causes of our time: *resilient, sustainable, regenerative, carbon negative*, still often lack the cohesiveness to

apply to specific needs, and indeed the potential of site specific design.

I came across a building located in Bilbao that I found hypnotic, and thinking back, it may have been the seed for my looking at location as a critical way in understanding contemporary high-performance design. If the Guggenheim Bilbao is a kind of spaceship coming from far away and landing next to the town center, then the Basque Health Department by Coll-Barreu Arquitectos transmutes the built environment around it, absorbing centuries of cultural archetypes into a new century formulation. Coll-Barreu Arquitectos conceived of a building on a downtown street corner that appears to be in the process of finding its final form, wrapped in black folds of glass with its mass-finding apogee at the building's edge. It is nine stories and utilizes two skins with a walkout between them. The facade captures the city in its fragments and projects them back into the public space. This simple gesture is an ocular ode to its dense surroundings, a celebration of the sky, street, neighboring buildings, and people passing by. If that was its singular design intention I would have quickly moved on, momentarily entertained by the images I found online. The gesture is in fact a multi-pronged response to a very constrained design criterion. Beginning with the Basque Health Department's need to interact with the citizens, the building's presence gives the organization a revitalized face to the public. Spending an afternoon photographing it I found myself being just as observant of all the movement around it, the sky above, and other photographers discovering the play of reflections. But a deeper thread emerges as the greater concerns were with how the building itself performs. By being perforated on the outside like a traditional Spanish elevated terrace, the interior maintains a connection to the city. Conversely, the outer skin protects from the sun, wind, and street noise to improve the quality and performance of the interior. It is an unapologetically contemporary and dense multi-use facility in the heart of a traditional community and is a complete response to conditions. I would soon discover that this wrapping gesture to incorporate multiple benefits into the facade is in fact found throughout Spain and frequently expressed in inventive ways.

Each region in this book expresses a distinct design sensibility and approach that excels in exploring the possibilities of a hyperlocalized architecture based on its unique conditions. The act of discovery is driven by the question of what challenges these projects solve. The topic is vast, rich, and fertile ground for designers who crave, and in fact, thrive on its challenges. We are no longer thinking of environmental design and sustainability as medicine but, instead, as nourishment. As basic design building blocks, this hyperlocalized architecture absorbs the cultural and natural elements around it and formulates them into gracious human habitats. It cleverly integrates resources like water, raw materials, sun, and energy. It reassesses program to congregate or reclaim, to connect, to learn, work or live in. The process of starting from place creates self-selecting design characteristics, which, once identified, are simple to recognize. In this way, place becomes a powerful lens for understanding the dynamic characteristics of how fully realized environmental architecture manifests.

Perhaps the most well-known building type represented here is Japan's micro housing movement, where highly crafted living experiences in very small spaces are using principles from centuries past to maximize the urban experience. The process of condensing architecture is vital to get right because the impending population growth and the evolution of cities will demand it. Germany has mastered building science to the degree that buildings of all sizes and locations will predictably use a small fraction of the energy a typical new building would. Dr. Wolfgang Feist's Passivhaus has spawned an entire design and building culture to implement deep building science principles at a large scale. Danish culture has adopted a collective form of design, which is, of course, all about the joy of the bicycle. Cascadia's embrace of native woods as the raw material for large-scale building puts them at the forefront of renewable building materials. Mexico is in its own early stages of exploring a contemporary form of low-impact design with notable projects built into the cool earth. Spain's embrace of high performance and design in commercial construction mixes the potential of light and program to provide beautiful articulations of wrapped form-making. Finally, there is Australia, where exuberant and daring ideas running the gamut of use are manifesting at an extraordinary rate. On a continent already threatened by uncontrolled global warming, the design community and its patrons are facing the challenge head-on with innovation and spontaneity. There is no perfect building, there is only the potential for the perfect response to existing conditions. Taken out of context, the projects lose their greatest asset. Put together, they create a new context, both within their own particular environments and with each other.

The suggestion of re-localizing design is neither new nor unusual, but has taken a backseat to a culture of celebrating the individual project without concern or meaning of its context. There are many ways for a project to lose its bearings and fall short of its potential. Camilla Block, design principal of Durbach Block Jaggers, states it plainly: "Because of the way buildings are chosen in an architecture competition, you have a split-second on a piece of paper to show what the idea is. So everything is nutshelled into these very simplistic one-liner interventions, and buildings are more complex than that. But the vehicle for getting buildings approved and projects through is not." This phenomenon has also translated seamlessly to online and print media, where the one-liner is effectively the design narrative. It's better to hook an audience in a cluttered media space with a big gesture than create a nuanced proposal which takes time to resolve its ideas. Could this lead to a design movement of buildings which are search engine optimized? Perhaps we are already at the piont where architecture is formulated for a digital landscape while making real world concerns secondary. Architecture schools often focus on the competence of a building to express something over how it responds to the given conditions. These studies can become shallow exercises that ignore the capacity of the site to provide core resources and add to the greater texture of community.

The flipside, which stunts creativity, is the tendency of the profession to go back to what has been done before because of the risk of alienating the owner, public, or perceived market expectations. The term value engineering has entered the lexicon of defining short-sighted goals based on upfront cost, to the detriment of long-term savings. This risk-adverse culture is slow to absorb core lessons emerging from the field.

The fact that any of the buildings on these pages have materialized is a testament to the ingenuity, persuasiveness, and commitment to a group of far-sighted practitioners and supporters. While risk taking is an underlying theme, the conversations here constantly come around to problem solving. The critical point of departure in designing for place is its intent. Architecture that mimics historical archetypes does a great disservice to advancing the capacity of the project in fulfilling contemporary needs with contemporary resolutions. Only by anticipating future conditions and using the best of what we understand here and now will we properly and fully embrace the challenges of environmental shaping. The next step is not just practicing contemporary design and methodologies but also actively challenging them. The way something looks is in service to how it performs, so taste becomes a distraction. This view is in correlation with the modernist aesthetic, only the design needs are environmental and not mechanistic. In this context, it really does not matter if a project is considered beautiful, quirky, or obnoxious. If the project's value is to serve humans and the environment equally and with skill, then current taste is a periphery exercise. If successful, these ideas become the templates for further investigations on more nuanced and important questions about our built environment's role in the natural environment. This process is clearly manifested with the wooden mid-rise Bullitt Center by Miller-Hull Architects, which achieved Living Building Challenge status in the solar energy–constrained urban center of Seattle. The design is fundamentally the summary of a very restrictive performance, resource, and material standard where each component has a direct lineage to the overall environmental goals. Or the opposite in both location and aesthetic is the Pixel Building in Melbourne, whose highly functional assets are flamboyantly asserted. The deeper lessons of the function of the project have given the firm studio 505 room to run with the concepts on much larger scales. Both projects are the vanguard of low impact technology and design but express that attribute via a visionary architecture born of where they are placed.

The guiding principles for selecting the projects for this book are how each one expresses the cutting edge of a design language of their region and how they relate to each other. An architecture sympathetic to the human requisite, and responsive to the natural condition. In the conversations the architects explain the building, the design process, and how they worked with the given conditions. There are many links among the dialogs, and while each is a meditation on the design process, together they become a query of where architecture can take us. By inserting a building into the fabric of a neighborhood or green field, there is the universal sense of healing. A building can become a catalyst for gathering like the Biblioteca de Can Llaurador and Commonwealth Place, or reinvent the neighborhood at a large scale like 8 Tallet and ANZ Centre. A building can outwardly be a commentary of its place like House Tokyo and Perforated House. A project can challenge an entire community's understanding of environmental design in the same way that the Pixel Building and the Bullitt Center do. Architecture can be restorative of biodiversity like the Ferrer Research & Development Center and the Van-Dusen Botanical Garden Visitor Centre.

Some of these buildings may or may not prove successful in the coming years and decades, and their influence can be difficult to quantify. It is remarkable, however, how each one can help inform the other, even if the architects are working independently. They create a break from mediocre, forced, or unfocused design habits. They embrace restraints as an agitator of creativity. As part of the vast impact we have on the natural environment they help pinpoint architecture's role in the face of an unprecedented and unambiguous process of climate change.

The first three conversations that follow frame the core considerations of environmental building design. Edward Mazria, Dr. Wolfgang Feist, and William McDonough each have unique insights into the issues of our built environment and have pioneered visionary solutions. They provide the framework for our capacity to resolve our singular challenge of climate and environmental degradation through design. The fact that we can talk about influencing at such scale is part of the ambitious and optimistic character of architecture. The lesson of hyper-localizing design is not to mimic or bluster, but to adapt to and challenge conditions. The scope of environmental building is extraordinary in its broad implications but because no two sites are the same, the process of exploring and embracing the specific attributes of a location and culture provides its own resolve. A great building is an elegant amalgam of conditions, with place as the catalyst.

Edward Mazria is the founder and director of Architecture 2030, Santa Fe, New Mexico. He has spearheaded multiple programs including the 2030 Challenge, 2030 District, and the 2030 Palette on-line design tool.

" In 2000, there was little discussion about architecture having anything to do with the climate issue. It wasn't until 2003, when *Metropolis* magazine published its Architects Pollute issue with the feature article titled, "Turning Down the Global Thermostat" that architecture and the built environment became recognized as the major contributors to the climate and energy crises and paradoxically, the sectors that could best solve them.

The notion of the building sector being a major contributor to carbon emissions originated in a workshop we conducted in our own architecture firm, bringing staff up to speed on the relationship of energy and the built environment. We conducted tutorials and one of the issues that came up was climate change, and "What does it have to do with us?" So we said, "Let's investigate, it's an interesting question." What we discovered was astonishing: buildings were consuming about 50% of all the energy produced and CO2 emitted in the United States.

Because of the way statistics were published, residential and commercial energy consumption (not including electricity), industrial and transportation energy consumption, and electricity-delivered energy and energy losses, there was no building sector component. What we did was create a true building sector operations number of about 43%, including residential and commercial building operations and building electricity consumption. Then we said what about building the buildings? And what about building materials like concrete, steel, and wood? We researched government studies completed in the 1980s, breaking out materials and construction as an embodied energy number for various building types. We then computed the embodied energy numbers into a building sector square foot average. "OK, we know how much new construction takes place each year," we said, so we multiplied annual building construction square footage and average embodied energy of building materials per square foot, and that came to 4% to 7% of total annual US energy

consumption, depending on the amount of building completed each year. So, approximately 43% annual US energy consumption is attributed to building operations, and 4% to 7% to building materials, for a total annual building sector percentage of about 50%.

Total embodied energy plus building operations is the total energy consumption of a building in any particular year. In year one, the total percentage of building energy consumption, before people walk in the door, is obviously 100% embodied energy, constructing the building and making its materials, and 0% is building operations. Now what happens over time is there's a crossover point. The total energy consumed by a building built today in the year 2030 is going to be divided equally between embodied energy and operation energy. And that's why building materials and construction is so important. If you want to reduce emissions between now and 2030 you must address the embodied energy issue as well as the operations energy consumption issue.

When we discovered that the building sector was responsible for about half of all energy consumption and emissions, we reframed the energy and climate change problem, and its solution. The scientific community, for example, frames the problem as burning fossil fuels leading to an increased concentration of greenhouse gases accumulating in the atmosphere. Its solution is to reduce emissions by substituting non-CO2-emitting energy sources. This puts the focus on the supply side of the issue. How much we're burning, projected to burn, and is left to burn, and how that will impact our planet.

At Architecture 2030, we look at the demand side of the built environment. By dramatically reducing demand, and through careful planning, design, and harnessing site renewable resources solar we can substantially eliminate the need to burn fossil fuels. Or, try to put the carbon emissions back in the ground, which is not going to happen any time soon, certainly not within the tipping-point time frame scientists are talking about.

In 2003, I made a cold call to *Metropolis* magazine after we discovered the building sector's contribution to the problem. At that time, transportation was the emissions story and SUVs were the poster child of America's excessive burning of fossil fuels. So, they were very skeptical at first about our building sector data, and it was contrary to a long-held belief in the architecture community that our work makes the world a better place and enhances people's lives. To say something like, "we are a global problem," is well, somewhat controversial. I pushed it a little bit and sent them the data. It took a few weeks but they got back to me saying they looked at the numbers and they checked out. One thing led to another and they said, "How about publishing a story in October, we'll send a writer out and give you the cover?"

Metropolis had the cover designed and chose the cover title "Architects Pollute." The issue came out in October 2003, created quite a stir in the profession, and grabbed national attention. Susan Szenasy, the editor of Metropolis, took some criticism when the issue first came out. It stirred things up, but architects, being who they are by training and temperament, are predisposed to do the right thing. They took up the cause, to problem solve, to create, and to make the world a better place.

Idealism is built into architectural education, into studio culture. It's one of the reasons people enter the field. So, when we issued the 2030 Challenge it took hold. The day we issued the Challenge in January 2006, the American Institute of Architects adopted it. That tells you something about the profession, its social commitment. They are the ones changing the world, building by building, and by developing and executing regional, city, district, and development plans.

Today, our planet is at 400 parts per million CO_2 in the atmosphere. We've already surpassed 350 ppm, the target for a relatively stable climatic system. We're in trouble, and our goal is to get us back to 350 ppm. To put what we are doing in context, let me run some numbers by you.

According to the Energy Information Administration (EIA), globally we're consuming about 542 Quadrillion BTU's (Quads) of energy annually. Eighty-three percent (83%) of that energy is from burning fossil fuels, 5.5% is nuclear energy, and 11.2% is from other sources. If we break out the other sources, hydroelectricity is 7.6%, and wind, solar, and geothermal add up to 3.6%. So, that's roughly 30 Quads nuclear, 41 Quads hydro, and 19 Quads wind, solar, and geothermal, or about 90 plus Quads out of the 542 Quads consumed globally today. Now, we're expected to increase our global energy consumption to 722 Quads by 2030; that's an additional 180 Quads. That's how much we'll need, given global population growth projections and the continuing migration of people into urban areas.

Globally, there is some hydroelectric power left to tap. The EIA estimates an increase of about 21 Quads of hydro by 2030. Then there's nuclear, but the next nuclear plant scheduled to come online, Finland's Olkiluoto 3, is seven years behind schedule and costing almost double its original price tag. The EIA estimates that nuclear power generation will increase 17 Quads by 2030, but I believe that's optimistic. That leaves wind, solar, and geothermal. The EIA estimates that wind, solar, and geothermal energy production will increase by about 19 Quads.

So, hydroelectricity, nuclear, wind, solar, and geothermal, non-CO_2-emitting energy production, is expected to increase 57 QBtu by 2030, but we are projected to need an additional 180 QBtu above the 542 QBtu we are now consuming. That is just to make up the difference in the increase. Even if we doubled the projected production of non-CO_2-emitting energy, which is highly unlikely, we can't even supply the increase.

We will not stop digging up fossil fuels, and we will not succeed in addressing climate change, unless we dramatically reduce energy demand, because people are going to go to work, shop, go to church, take vacations, and heat, light, and cool their homes, offices, grocery stores, malls, and airports. There will be huge pressure to keep all that running. What we can do is design a built environment that consumes less energy in a smarter way. Look what happened in Greece when the government raised taxes 450% on heating oil. Many Greeks returned to wood burning, illegally logging and removing trees in national and city parks. They were burning whatever they could get their hands on. If you have that kind of economic and climatic pressure, people will look to satisfy short-term needs. All of this is doubly unfortunate because Greece has a mild climate ideal for passive heating; it would be easy and preferable to incorporate passive design systems rather than damage the local environment. In 2003, I said architects are the problem and the solution. Look, some degree of climate change appears inevitable. Whether it is manageable or catastrophic, however, will not be determined in Washington, or Geneva, or Beijing, or by legislation and international treaties, or by silver bullet energy technologies, but by how we, the architecture, planning, and building community respond and act.

There's a misconception out there that high-performance buildings cost more, or that clients, or contractors, or city governments, or financial institutions control the design process. Make no mistake, architects control how and what they design. They conceptualize a building and select the systems and materials that go into it. That, right there, determines 60% to 80% of a building's energy consumption. Things like the siting of a building, its shape, color, and orientation, the location and size of fenestrations, materials and their properties, and the systems and equipment that go into a building. Architects conceptualize, design, and specify the thousands of parts and materials that give a building form and make it function. And they make hundreds of decisions and choices along the way—for each decision or choice, there are hundreds, maybe thousands of available options. Building design is a complex process of tradeoffs to meet a specific

program and project budget. As long as architects bring a project in on budget, they have great flexibility in what they design and specify. They can design an efficient or inefficient building for the same cost.

If we incorporate best practices, those planning and design strategies outlined in the 2030 Palette, the reductions will be even greater and we will meet the 2030 Challenge targets. The 2030 Palette provides the guiding principles for this solution-oriented approach. Putting these principles into practice can also alleviate the political and economic pressure to dig up and burn unconventional fossil fuel reserves like shale oil and gas.

The 2030 Palette is an interactive online tool that puts the principles behind low-carbon and resilient built environments at the fingertips of architects, planners, and designers worldwide. Our goal is to inform the planning and design process at the point of inspiration. By curating the best information, and using powerful visuals and straightforward language, highly complex ideas are made intuitive and accessible. Guiding principles are presented as individual "swatches," which together make up the larger fabric of sustainable built environments. Swatches are both global in scope and local in practice, providing location-specific strategies for applications across the built environment, from interconnected transportation and habitat networks that span entire regions, to elegant passive design applications that can daylight, heat, or cool a building. The platform will continue to grow with new content and features added as transformation of the built environment unfolds.

US and global economies are picking up, so construction is also picking up. Over the next two decades, 900 billion square feet of building will be built and rebuilt in urban areas around the world. It is imperative that we plan, design, and build differently. Over the next two decades, most of the global built environment will be either new or rebuilt. This is our opportunity, one with a defined window that will not remain open indefinitely. The time to act is now. 🙟

Edward Mazria

DR. WOLFGANG FEIST

Dr. Feist is the founder and director of the Passivhaus Institut, Darmstadt, Germany. He lives and teaches in Innsbruck, Austria.

" The main principle behind Passive House is to look at what we call the energy services. This is what you really want in a building to stay comfortable. You want conditions to be as healthy as possible inside; you want to have fresh air, daylighting, and things like that. So these are the conditions defining what you want to design for. This is worldwide, based mainly because of two facts: the first is that the physics ruling all of this is the same everywhere, and the second fact is that the comfort people want to have is also the same. Therefore, the inside is almost always at the same conditions, although there are cultural differences that one has to account for, of course.

What is not the same are the external conditions—we have different climates. What is also not the same is the cultural heritage, so there are different ways to construct a building. So that led us to a performance-based standard looking at these climatic conditions on the inside. These inside conditions give as a very simple kind of equipment, what is really needed. The outside conditions define the kind of effort we have to take to reach the goal of thermal comfort.

It's a completely different approach from what has been done in the past where you just do your envelope to separate the inside from the outside and then in order to create a tolerable climate inside you apply additional technology. When your design is based on the technology to create an adequate climate the construction of a high-rise glazed tower in Sydney and in Hong Kong and Jakarta is the same as the one in Montréal. That of course will give you very high energy consumption in different climates for different reasons, because it's too cold or it's too hot or you have too much of solar radiation. Additional technology can correct for these errors, so that allowed one to create basically one design and bring it in by helicopter to the different sites.

That was the kind of thinking that happened all through the world, and it is completely the opposite of a Passive House. It's only possible, because energy was thought to be and to stay extraordinarily cheap.

With the Passive House, we accept our need for a perfect interior climate, so now based on the local climate, our envelope has to be designed in order to be able to use a very low-impact technology on the inside. Such a concept of course leads to different types of solutions in the different climates. That's what many people find hard to understand and they state, "We have to redefine passive house for different climates." But no, we don't, because it's the same equation, the same underlying physics. It is the solutions that are looking very different depending on the climate and depending on the boundary conditions in the individual circumstances.

This is how we understood it when we first began because this is how physicists think. We think in general terms and try to find a general rule or principle behind it. That is a good idea to do that in this way because now you can decentralize, we now know the method for the solutions, which can be found in every place relatively easily if the method is once figured out. That's what the scientists at the Passive House Institute have done, and they made the method with a very simple tool available for everybody. It turns out that given the limited technology that people had in the past of course they did a good job with regional traditional design. There have been different types of architectural heritage in different parts of the world, and of course it had something to do with the local climate. They knew how to build for the local climate given the technology at that time. Technology has changed now, and this is also something we have to take into account, we are not against modern technology; on the contrary, we should use modern technology, but use it in a wise way. It is still good to reduce the overall amount of additional technology because in the end it will not provide satisfactory results. You can see that in most buildings now where there are over exaggerated technological solutions for the indoor climate. Buildings that were never adapted to the place that they were built only to rely on these systems. What I think about technology is that it should be used in a clever and responsible way. That's

not easy because sometimes people just love the complex things. And there is another tendency in an industrialized society to keep things the way it has been. Some of the complicated things we have kept I think have been artificially designed by the chance that technology has taken.

When you reflect back on what we did with Passive House, it is not as difficult as you envision at the first moment. It's about the difference between what is done normally, like for windows where we go from a single pane of glass to three—that seems to be a big step, but a few years later it just becomes normal. It's normal because this is not complicated, it is not difficult, it is just different.

I believe that Passive House has worked because firstly it all has to be based on solid science, speculation does not help. You need to be skeptical and you need to scrutinize what you are doing. A lot of people just advertise what they want to sell and people are somewhat fed up with that. And then there has to be a demonstration so that you can see that it is working. You need to build it and it needs to work. That's why the science behind it has to be resilient; and you need to do it everywhere, not just in one place. You need people who are enthusiastic about it and engaged and you need to communicate about it. This is how our institute works, we work on the scientific level and we disseminate. Everything we have done so far has been published. We don't just publish on a scientific level but in formats for craftsman, architects, engineers, and others to use it for their own work. I am very positive about this and maybe that's an attitude of physicists. We have seen from theory that this is possible, and from actual development we have seen it's really working.

The Heat Recovery Ventilation manufacturers, for instance, had been very skeptical at the beginning but now some have certified almost all their units. They realized that these performance numbers are exactly what you need to be in the market. They realized that because our testing methodologies are based on real conditions in real houses.

There is more sophisticated software on the market but the Passive House Planning Package (PHPP) has gained so much attention because we always introduced the experience from the realized projects in order to find the boundary conditions for the calculations, so you can rely on what you are calculating. This has helped participants gain confidence in the system. The software needs to reflect the boundary conditions, to be as close to the average behavior as possible. For real construction you should be able to trim those variables like insulation thickness or internal heat loads. In principle, it is an easy thing but often architects are not involved in this so they sometimes hesitate in designing for it. I'm a fan of dynamic simulation, and we normally have a bunch of variables 200, 300, 400, and you might think that you can change one or another but it becomes very dangerous because some of these you can't vary in reality. This leads to surprises and a lot of uncertainty. The problem is "garbage in, garbage out," so if you get the variables wrong, even as physicists sometimes we got it wrong. So if we were simply pea counting—the more we have the more easy it is to get it wrong. To see the big picture is the important thing, it's not about every pea. It's about understanding what the important issues are. That is what we tried to implement in the PHPP.

I do define myself as a student of nature. Scientists like Carl Sagan, Bill Nye, or Neil deGrasse Tyson, demonstrate the kind of thinking that is positive, it brings us forward. And it is also about reflecting on the change that humankind might influence the natural world. We have to be cautious with that. This was forgotten in the first Industrial Revolution, it was not so important then—but now it is. We as humankind can do so many things, among them we can destroy this world. We have to constrain ourselves not to do so. When I say destroy the world, I mean of course, that biology will go on but, what we will destroy is the human habitat. As Carl Sagan said, "We are a way of the Cosmos to know itself." Wouldn't that be a mess to destroy it?

When you think back in history the first scientists like Galileo, Newton, and Alexander von Humboldt, they thought about the conscience you get from science. They thought about the spiritual component to science, it was not simply about technology. It is not bad to create technology but it is very necessary to reflect on its impact. Now science is industrialized where it is used to develop new products and to service industry. There are two impacts as a result. The first being that it is getting boring, it's just about money like everything else. But there is much more to science of course than money, it is about getting to know how things work, it is fun. The other side is that of course it is important to act responsibly. So, if there are two paths to getting good indoor climate, one is using fossil fuels and the other path is just insulating your building better then I think there is no choice which path to go.

I think most people don't understand that yet, it seems to be a little too abstract. But when they see the building that only consumes 10% of the energy they are surprised and wonder how that can be. I think this is because they have been told their whole life that the more energy you have the better your living standard is. Now we understand that it's about how clever you can do things and that you can provide this with very little energy "demand," what is just the part of the energy, you are losing to the environment.

It seems that people may need a gentle reminder of the big picture from time to time, and I am open to engage that way. What we really want to emphasize is to have these grassroots developments, which take off. I would like to see them create solutions in their environment, and it is very satisfying to see that this is possible. The solutions we have looked for are not so difficult—it can be done. It can even be done by a farmer in Namibia building a straw bale Passive House building. This may not be the solution in the US or Europe, but it could be the solution in some places. So, distributing the science behind it can help to find local solutions that are much better than what they had before.

And then there are projects that are about scale like Heidelberg-Bahnstadt, which is a very good model for industrialized high-density urban development. I very much enjoyed walking inside the development because it is all pedestrian. You can send your children to the playground and you won't have to worry about them crossing a busy street for instance. In a project like this it already changes the attitudes. Now, often what we talk about is technological, but these things change the general attitude. Passive House is only a small part of this: there are things that are more critical like the pedestrian area. But, it did instill confidence that a low impact community can work.

Climate change is an existential crisis. There are species that are dying out right now because of human activity. I do not like this, but we might be able to live as a planetary society with a fraction of the existing species. If we heat up the planet 6°C it is a problem for our industrial society because we won't be able to live the way we do now. This is why we have to change the path; there have to be solutions for this problem. This will have to be resolved either way, by design or by warfare with people fighting over resources. They won't be conscious of why they're fighting. It quickly becomes just a fight—and people lose their minds, like they have done in wars throughout history. I am convinced that we have to resolve this problem before things get really nasty. So this is why we should not have arguments about whether it is better to insulate or to install solar, we need both. Sometimes I'm a little bit surprised about this infighting between different approaches. I know that we need to be very tolerant.

It is important to think about designing issues with the least impact possible, and in most cases it means thinking local. Let's look at energy again; we can create locally produced energy, which we are incorporating into our standards. The more localized you try to make your primary energy the more time dependence becomes an issue. So you have some days with enough sun so that you don't need to heat, but there are other days that are cloudy where you need to heat but you don't have solar energy. If you have a network which is maybe even a thousand kilometers connecting different environments, it becomes much easier. In this way, it is good for a society to work together to create such networks, not everything has to be localized. But we have to keep the rights on the network in the hands of the society relying on it. That is already working in Europe. It is about using the right technology because people always thought that they were dependent on this big scale energy infrastructure. And now they realize that no, we are not. It becomes less centralized and more adapt for the needs of the people. So with Passive House, the solutions are geared for the way the building is used where the building is built.

The background is still science, but if you try to get to that at just an experimental level it won't work because it takes too long. That would be evolution the hard way. Now we can simulate these things, and run many experiments at the same time on the computer. Imagine how many buildings we would have to build to get this information? So this is where the new science can come in and help us in that responsible way, and the important thing is to make that available for everybody. That's the concept behind what we do. That the PHPP, for instance, is on an Excel spreadsheet, makes it very affordable, and you can have fun learning it. The energy model provides immediate feedback so you can see what the effects are of what you do. Physicists have always worked this way—this is why it's fun to do physics. This is a new approach, and I think it will help because it also has an educational part. That is because in the end, you get the big picture. It's not a thing in which you have to rely on an expert, it empowers the way you can design a building. Once built we can measure how the Passive House performs, that's when people feel empowered and not just dependent on some experts. In the end, I believe this will be the biggest change. Going back to Carl Sagan, this is that idea that we all have the capacity to understand science. 🙿

William McDonough heads the architecture practice McDonough + Partners, Charlottesville, North Carolina. He is also the co-founder of the Cradle to Cradle Institute, MBDC, and Make it Right Foundation.

" When we first wrote Cradle to Cradle we said in the book, "Waste equals food, use current solar income, and respect diversity." We decided to get rid of the word "waste" because if you use the word waste you're accepting that it exists. So we don't even use it, instead we call it nutrients. That's why I don't believe in sewer treatment in cities, I believe in nutrient management. Treatment is where you add nasty things to sewage then dump them into the bay. So, instead of sewage treatment I look at them as phosphate, nitrogen, methane, et cetera, that are fertilizer factories and eliminate point source pollution at the cities so that the bays comes back with shellfish and so forth. The fertilizer goes to the farmers in the country who use it as slow-release which then gets rid of non-point source pollution. Every time you have a downpour you don't have a non-point source going into the Chesapeake Bay creating algae blooms for instance. It's beautiful because the city starts to heal the country and the country heals the city and feeds it. It goes back into symbiosis. When I was a baby in Tokyo, farmers came to collect our sewage at night. I always thought the city and the farms were one organism, and I still do.

So instead of saying waste equals food, we say everything is food—food for life and food for technology, because we have these two protocols for metabolism: biological and technical. And food for thought is important because it's about endless resourcefulness. To have biological and technical materials in metabolism means the city and the country are one big thing continually exchanging materials. These are creative acts, so it's not just the materials that are resources but also human creativity.

We also don't say to use "solar income" because we are now seeing new forms of energy that are not solar and it's very exciting. The last is we changed "respect diversity" to "celebrate diversity," because you can respect something while it's dying. You can respect the monarch butterfly while its habitat collapses. We say celebrate because now I'm bringing the butterflies back. That's different.

I see assets where others see liabilities. I'm always on the search on how this can be a "goodness" rather than a "badness" or a "less badness." The value of a tool is assigned by the intension of the human using the tool. So is a hammer a good or bad? Well, depends if I hit you in the face or if I build your house. Is nanotechnology good or bad? It's just a tool. Nano bombers on your ceiling killing people for religious reasons or whatever would be pretty scary. But nanobots going into your artery to clean out some plaque might be a nice prospect. The tool's value is placed there by our intentionality.

What happens just on the mobility front gets very exciting because the next thing you know we have the kind of bus transit that Jaime Lerner did in Curitiba. If you think about that it's actually about how you love children in a city in a funny way because he created a whole new form of currency, which was mobility. They couldn't get into the favelas to take out the trash so he said, look, if you bring it out, including the children, and put it somewhere where we can get it, we will pay you in transit tokens. Now you can go get a job, wow. So instead of the city paying for garbage collection, they created a mobility system for people who couldn't afford it so they can get to wherever they want to go. It's an integrated, low-cost solution with benefits everywhere and everyone wins. Everyone can get around without a car. For food, take the low-lying areas, which are flooded, he said don't live there because they're dangerous, so he made them into city gardens and farms. If you don't have any food for your family, you can get on the public transit and work on a farm and you can be paid in food. You get enough to feed your family healthy organic food, get on the transit and go home. And it keeps people from squatting in the lower areas, which is dangerous. It's so beautiful.

These things are hard to do, but we are innovators. I think two years ago there was a report that there was $9 billion worth of sustainability consulting. If you price it out you realize it's $9 billion of scorekeeping. These are all scorekeepers, like who has the sharpest tool to reduce your carbon. So it would be like going to a soccer game and going there to watch the scorekeepers. Really? Is that the exciting part, watching the scoreboard? No, you want to watch the game. What is the game? It's people on the field making mistakes, falling down, getting back up, kicking the ball. What's amazing is that it's a team innovating at high speed, falling down getting back up, but they know where the goal is. That's the game, that team knows that goal. That's what improv is, but it's also pure innovation at high-speed. That's fun to watch.

We are not here to tweak the system that's wrong in the first place. We don't go in and say, "Oh, we can do our zoning a little bit better." I go in and say, "Wait a minute; with Cradle to Cradle you do not need zoning because my factories are not dangerous. I designed textiles where the water coming out of the mills is clean enough to drink. What am I afraid of?" So I'm looking at architecture and I'm doing it for the kids, as long as it's safe. If you want to work in it go ahead; if you to want have an apartment make it an apartment. Now we have a critical mass of people to make it work for retail. So the buildings get designed for continuous use and optimized utility for multiple generations. Why would I want zoning? Why would I want an office park with residential towers that are three miles away?

When Toyota puts an ad out and they say their aim is zero emissions, it's not even good science. Let's have something that makes oxygen. If we had trees that made zero emissions we would all be dead. Why wouldn't you want buildings like trees? When you think of it like that then it's rather obvious. This is all based on human creativity, and the ability for us to advance and continuously improve with freedom from the remote tyranny of bad design. Why should I be tyrannized about yesterday's bad decision? It would be like playing football and being trapped by the last play, like you have to keep playing it over and over again. That is the most boring game. It's much

more fun to improvise, constantly. That's why the cultural question becomes interesting because at that point the culture can express itself in a creative way. It still has integrity because you're expressing yourself creatively within a context. You're solving for rich, local problems. All sustainability, like politics, is local. It has to be.

As we work on our new sewage treatment systems, for instance, I don't care if we end up designing equipment that gets made anywhere. At the end when you say, oh all the jobs are where they are making this equipment somewhere else and we lose our jobs here, the answer is no. If you do these things correctly all this equipment can only be deployed at a local level. Interestingly, what happens is production can be brought to you at less cost because of industrialization and coherent supply chains that are optimizing, allowing communities everywhere to take on their own nutrient management. That nutrient management is inherently local. The Chinese cannot capture the sewage of St. Louis. It's the same with solar. Everyone worries about who makes the solar collectors. Sure, these are disruptive times and we are commoditizing these things. Now at 80 cents a watt, the solar collectors are a commodity. Hallelujah, because wherever it gets deployed, the Chinese will not capture an American photon. They are at the local level. That is what happens.

The most important resources around us, though, are the creativity of our children and goodwill. If you don't have those two the rest of it is noise. We have one fundamental design question when we start a project: "How do I love all the children of all the species for all the time." That's it. So whenever we are working on something everyone in the office can breathe and go, "Hmmm, how does this love all the children of all the species for all the time?" All of a sudden you go, oh!

I'll give you an example. We were asked by the Annenberg Foundation in Los Angeles to assist in a project, which turned out to be quite an interesting puzzle. The Navy had a development that has been derelict for 15 years. At the time, many women were returning from Afghanistan and many were traumatized by their military deployment. They wanted to provide this housing, which was a good idea, but they couldn't do it because the environmentalists were blocking it. This was now one of the last, if not the last, habitats of the Palos Verdes Blue butterfly. I think it got down to something like 150 individuals. That's it. This is an endangered species for sure. They're saying you can't come back and occupy the space.

This is the famous story that plays itself out in so many places with endangered species. They said, "Bill, can you come in and help?" This is a quandary because on one hand we want to save the butterfly, and on the other these women can benefit from this place. What we did is actually funny—we decided to celebrate everybody. The Navy men get to fly around in jets as the Blue Angels, so what if we call the women coming back the Blue Butterflies? In fact, they are the same thing, they're both endangered and they need each other. And what if we help the kids understand that instead of having a lawn with sprinklers, what if we had butterfly habitats instead. What if we teach everyone what it means to have a butterfly habitat and track them with a smartphone? What if we celebrate how many butterflies we have, and how many more we can have, instead of how many are left? What if we galvanize the small community around the restoration of the women's enjoyment of the world and the blue butterflies? Let's have a little joint pavilion for anybody, where we can have a movie night where people can come together as a community. When no one else is there, it can sense your presence and tells you the story of the Palos Verdes Blue butterfly. So the butterfly becomes the point, it's this thing that changes the way you see. The first job of the designer is not to build or to rearrange the furniture, it's to change the way you see. So let's start there.

They don't have less damage to the habitat, which is what they were trying to do. Instead they have an increase in habitat. There are now these children out there who have their whole life ahead of them, who are in love with this little butterfly because that is who they are. Falling in love with another species is so important. You know people love dogs, they love their cats, or their horses, and they can love their butterflies. You are not only connecting them with something larger, they also need love. That's why in Cradle to Cradle we design things in three categories. There are the things you need, food and vehicles for instance. There are the things you want which would be a high-performance car. And then there's what you love, which for me is a 1958 Mercedes-Benz Roadster Cabriolet that I can take out every Sunday. Need, want, love. Love all children, all species, for all time, what a wonderful place to live. And then work your way back to need. So there are women needing a place to live, and they want a decent place to raise children. And I love the place they live and I love the children and they love all the species where they live. Now we are cooking.

It's local, so I ask, where are you? There are places that don't need any help at all with this, like Bali. It's just natural. There are places like Curitiba, which started with Jaime Lerner and was an amazing inspiration for me. When Jamie started there were maybe 600,000 people, now it's probably close to 3 million. The dynamics change now with these various issues but what an astonishing thing he did there. One of the things I find delightful is working in the Netherlands. They look at nature as something in which they are critically engaged and they have to be in a positive relationship with it, they have no choice. If you live 15 feet below sea level you get pretty serious about it. It's a culture that had to work together. You are in symbiosis with the forces: wind and gravity. The rest of it to me is the necessity of clues. There are clues everywhere in different places. 🙶

CASCADIA

HARVESTS]

[BULLITT CENTER]

[VANDUSEN BOTANICAL GARDEN VISITOR CENTRE]

As cities grow in height and density, the expectation of buildings to find a synergy with the environment is shifting from an abstract ideal to a design challenge. Consider, for instance, the notion that a building that is renewable by design is in fact harvested. The culling of biomass for the raw materials of construction provides a link between the built environment and the abundant natural processes of regeneration. Edward Mazria speaks about the stunning projected growth in demand for new buildings, where 75% will either be new or go through a major retrofit by 2035, which is a churn rate of 8% of the world's building stock every year. The question becomes, what can we possibly build with that does not inject massive amounts of CO2 into the sky? Instead, CO2 is captured from the air using photosynthesis, and becomes a basic building block. We can introduce it into our cities in the form of cellulose fibers working in tension, and impregnated with a lattice of lignin, which resists compression. Wood is in fact so ubiquitous and central to small building design that it is easy to forget its history and overlook its potential to do much greater things. In 30 years, or perhaps much sooner, a wooden sky-scraper will be commonplace.

Buildings, then cities, made out of wood become our carbon bank. A 2014 study *Carbon, Fossil Fuel, and Biodiversity Mitigation With Wood and Forests* from Yale University explores how the carbon savings of wood harvesting for construction works in two distinct ways. The first is the avoidance path. Heavy timber building would reduce the CO2 emissions of construction 14% to 31% by avoiding the burning of fossil fuels to produce steel and concrete, which themselves contribute a total of 10% to humanity's total atmospheric carbon. Secondly, carbon tied up in the wood is 1/2 of the total weight of the material, locked away for the life of the building. This storage path overcomes the difficult hurdle of developing methods to decarbonize

construction. The exhaustive study of studies demonstrates how harvesting our forest's biomass sequesters carbon at a much greater capacity than leaving forests untouched because of the relatively large amounts of C02 young trees can absorb compared to older trees. These small trees become the source materials for engineered lumber.

Now the conversation pivots from sustainability to adaptability by re-localizing the materiality of buildings. The Pacific Northwest region, roughly from British Columbia to Oregon, is often referred to as Cascadia and has a distinctive socio-environmental ethic that provides the perfect template to explore and express the potential of heavy timber construction on a large scale. Wood was the core industry for much of the Northwest a century ago; downtown Seattle and Vancouver both began as logging operations in the mid 1800s. The term "skid row" is derived from the main path where logs were taken to the mills, and the sprouting working-class neighborhoods alongside. The explosive growth of western cites was born on the strength of timber. Many of the brick-clad multi-story offices and warehouses in Seattle and Vancouver have a heart of massive timber posts and beams holding them up for 100 years or more. But as the forest waned and modernity introduced new technologies, building large structures with wood became a forgotten heritage. When I visited Miller Hull's offices in downtown Seattle, I was surprised to see they occupied the top floor of a six-story nearly century–old all wood tower. These buildings are ubiquitous and often well loved, but not seen as part of the advancement of modern tall construction like the early towers of Chicago and New York, where steel lacing concrete cores ushered in the modern urban forest.

Now there is an abrupt and considerable interest in large wood construction. The advent of glul-ams, Cross-Laminated Timbers (CLT), Laminated Veneer Lumber (LVL), and other systems has re-energized the architectural understanding of renewable materiality. Because wood is a structurally significant, but uniquely plastic material, it is easily adaptable for creating complex forms. The advancement in engineered timbers comes from using smaller stock and pressing and gluing the raw material into much larger units. Glulams are the most well known type, consisting of 2x board stock glued latterly to create enormous beams. CLTs are a derivative, the timbers are glued parallel on each layer to become large structural panels. LVLs and similar systems use strands of wood pressed with glue under intense heat and pressure to create beams.

Wooden towers are on the drawing board by Vancouver-based architect Michael Green that reach 30 stories. Skidmore, Owings & Merrill and a host of other large firms are now following suit. Austrian-based developer CREE GmbH is among a growing list of construction groups that offer turnkey timber towers that can be erected in days, and large-scale timber construction is now a familiar proposal in building design competitions and proposals worldwide. As codes and the public views of timber construction adapt, the technology will be embraced for the economic and environmental impacts. Using design and engineering know-how and construction infrastructure already in place, wooden engineering systems are a fungible technology. In other respects, wood outperforms other materials in seismic areas and during fires due to how predictable it moves and burns.

Wood may seem like a poor substitute as the world's biomass and habitat is in decline, and in some regions like equilateral zones, critical, but forests are expanding in other regions. The resource is not only bountiful in places like Cascadia but crucial as northwestern larch, pine, and fir forests are picked clean by the infestation of pine bark beetles and large fire events that leave vast supplies of lumber on the ground rotting. Many soft wood forests are also burdened with too many trees, as a result of a legacy of overly eager fire suppression, which ironically creates a much more significant fire hazard as suppression leaves the forest understory choked with fuels.

Historically, the logging industry left a detrimental scar on millions of acres of ancient woodlands. The old heavy timber buildings were made from beams and posts of those massive logs, a practice unheard of today. This rampant culling of the best trees left a gaping hole in the land, quickly swallowed up by smaller, much denser stands. These second- and third-generation forests are merely a ghost of what the pre-industrialized landscapes evolved into over millennia. Ninety percent (90%) of the old growth stands in the US are lost, water absorption reduced on the denuded lands drastically changed the local climate and spillways, and a host of natural phenomena and biodiversity disrupted is the hallmark of a century and half of clear cutting.

The harvesting of wood can either continue to be a major environmental gash or become a restorative action. While green certification of raw materials is still a rarity in the manufacturing industry, the Forest Stewardship Council, founded in 1993, has made a successful case that responsible and economically viable materials sourcing is possible at an impactful scale. A soundly managed and harvested forest is diverse in the age of trees, with openings in dense forest stands providing habitat for plants which become food for animals and insects, and these forests are better adapted to future fires and climate change. Plantations and forests already culled can be harvested every decade and half because the wood does not need to be from large trees to make modern engineered wood structural products. Because young trees absorb carbon the most readily, along with biochar they provide the greatest opportunity humans currently have to sequester carbon at any appreciable scale.

ARCHITECT
MILLER HULL PARTNERSHIP
SEATTLE, UNITED STATES
2013
4,645 SQUARE METERS
LIVING BUILDING CHALLENGE

[BULLITT CENTER]

Designed to be fully self-supporting in the heart of the growing urban section in the east side of Seattle's famous Capitol Hill neighborhood, the Bullitt Center is the region's first heavy timber tower built in 80 years. The project was designed under the Living Building Challenge (LBC) protocol, meaning that nearly every aspect in its design was considered for the health and environmental impacts. The building's altruistic design is intended to prove the viability of deep sustainable goals in an urban setting. It pushes the very limits of what is possible within the constraints of a municipality.

The implication of harvesting goes well beyond materials as the building produces more energy than it consumes, supplies its own water from reclamation and rain capture, and even recycles the human effluent on-site. The four-story timber core on top of a two-story concrete base satisfies a number of environmental goals while being economically and technically practical. The massive solar array is the most aggressive aspect of an otherwise outwardly utilitarian restraint. The aesthetics of the project are resolved, or better yet, settled by the robust metrics and methods of the LBC and the requirement to meet an ambitious 250-year use cycle. Developed by the Bullitt Foundation to inspire the possibilities of what is often referred to as *regenerative design*, the project's core lesson is the benefits of allowing form to follow function.

BRIAN COURT

"Miller Hull has always said we are trying to do a richer modernism. Buildings that people like more, buildings that are tied to the community, that are regionally derived and are regional solutions to problems.

I think it is embedded in the Miller Hull approach to try to simplify buildings and try to put them together elegantly so you can express the mechanical systems, express structural systems, and give the building a sort of layering and depth. You don't have to add all these expensive finishes afterward. In respect to wood, early on we were looking at concrete, steel, and heavy timber. Concrete was the early odds-on favorite because of the thermal mass. It would help us create a more passive, stable building. It was also going to give us a thin floor-plate assembly, which would also give us more natural lighting. Steel had all kinds of liabilities, the fireproofing that was required—you're wrapping all the columns because steel on its own is not fire resistant. Either we have to use intumescent paint, which is expensive, or spray on fireproofing, then wrap it in drywall. The finishes are usually where you get most of the toxins in building materials, so the more we could minimize finishes going into the building, the better off we were going to be as far as the Living Building Challenge red list.

We work with heavy timber a lot because there are great environmental benefits and it is a regional resource. We have a lot of timber in the Northwest and it is available. We liked it also because there is no finishing required once the frame goes in; there is no drywall, taping, or mudding. We just leave it, express it, and it brings warmth to the building. The Bullitt Center is a heavy timber building so all that structure needs is a one hour burn rating, meaning the columns and beams had to be a minimum size. The floor had to have a minimum of

2.5 inches of wood so if we used 2x4 and 2x6 construction like old warehouses, we could span 10 feet. With just the decking, we had something similar to a concrete structure with a topping slab that could span it. I often say there is a lot of new school stuff in this building, but there is also a lot of old school stuff as well. I think this is the first heavy timber multi-story building permitted in the city for 80 years.

There's a lot to talk about heavy timber systems. Typical steel bucket connections don't pass the fire code, so you typically use steel knife plates inside the timbers for protection. That is much more expensive, and we had to get the contractor on board because we had an integrated system all the way through, so when we said sealed connectors a red flag went up. We had to work on a simpler and easier system. We talked to the fire marshal and they wanted to have each beam with direct bearing on the column below, but wood can move a lot in construction, and shrink up to a half inch per floor. That is due to cross-grain loading, but the wood in the axial position does not move at all. So we have tube steel connectors, which go from the bottom of one column to the top of the next, and are a bit smaller so the beam rests directly on the column. This also allows the contractor to have the beams cut off-site, bring them in and drop them into these buckets.

The wood beams are an interesting problem. Because they are wood members glued together using a formula that has formaldehyde in it, there is not a glue that has structural integrity right now that is soy-based, for instance, and the Living Building Challenge will grant you an exception on the red list because there is no way to achieve the goals. The alternative is to go to solid sawn timber, using bigger older trees, so glulams are great because

they are smaller sticks of wood and everything is FSC certified. If forests are well-managed and productive, then what is the ultimate building material really? Timber construction is tried and true. I would be most concerned with concrete construction. How is a concrete building going to perform in a seismic event? With timber you can see it all, if a beam is checking, gets damaged, or there is a fire, you can shore it up or replace it. By pulling structure inside the envelope, you take a burden off that structure because now it's in a conditioned space. That piece is going to last 250 years. But, say you only get 75 years out of the skin, you can still replace the curtain wall. Solar panels in the electric blinds are the easiest to replace. Everything is layered.

Denis Hayes, president of the Bullitt Foundation, has really been a driving force. He was at every design meeting and has been intimately involved all the way through. He wants to change the way we think about construction and what will have the most significant and measurable effect on the built world. Let's go that far and commit to it. To do a six-story, solar-powered building in Seattle, which has all these other requirements, means there are a lot of things to work through. The project has had a lot of criticism for its budget, but it's a prototype. We have to literally reinvent the wheel every step of the way. The materials red list was probably the toughest, as everything that goes into the building has to have a materials data sheet and be vetted. Some things are proprietary. You're supposed to be doing things as close to the site as possible, so every time you think you found a solution to the red list, now you may be out of the travel radius.

US manufacturers did not have what we needed in terms of a low U-value of 0.25

glazing in the curtain wall for instance. Schüco is a German product that was way outside of the radius, but they saw it as a great opportunity to set up a West Coast presence. They shipped dyes over and had a local aluminum extruder pull the sticks up in Everett. The glass is also manufactured locally, which is a triple glazed, thermally broken curtain wall system. The entire window opens vertically off the wall so that the window compresses the weather stripping evenly. And because it opens high and low, you get better ventilation.

For daylighting, we wanted a thin floor plate at the perimeter so we could get our windows as close to the ceiling as possible. We ended up using a concrete topping slab which helps us heat and cool the building via a ground source heating and cooling loop and radiant tubing. So it is cooling the building on hot days in July and August with a hybrid system. Ninety percent (90%) of the work is done by the in-slab system, and since we need makeup air in the office spaces, we were required to have an HVAC system, which we could use for added cooling. We talked a lot about natural cooling but when we went to the hydronic system it made a lot of sense.

To be net zero energy we had to be in operation for a year. With design and engineering alone, we did not achieve our energy goals, so occupant behavior is critical, like taking the stairs instead of the elevator. Denis from the very beginning was asking from us what he called, "an irresistible stair," a stair that would keep people out of the elevator. From the stairs you get the best view of downtown and the Olympic Mountains. You can see the constructed wetland for rain reclamation. Denis said that each facade of the building had to respond to different conditions so each should look different, but in the

end we treated them all the same because we have an external blind system that modulates the light. Light shelves don't work in the Pacific Northwest because overcast skies are the dominant weather condition.

While we used many of these practices and technologies before, we never used them all in one place. We try to make the most responsible decision every time as you couldn't just solve one problem. Because everything is so connected, it will effect two or three other disciplines. Everything is interdependent much like a natural organism. It's interesting because it can't all just be engineering and science-based, there is still this human component. There is this blending of art and science. It becomes more like a natural organism, which is inherently beautiful. If people don't love the building, it does not matter how high performing it is, they don't want to be there.

An office building is pretty boring to look at, but this one has a glass stair and you can see people moving up and down, showing the building has a life. The building now has a dialog with the community because all these eyes are down on the sidewalk instead of the elevator shaft. It helps the community of the building as well because now occupants are bumping into each other to stop and have a chat. You sacrifice a little bit of your office space, but there's this big gain for the community that's using the building. And like the solar panels, or constructed wetlands, which take the function of the building to the outside, we express those functions and those functions become the architecture. We're not bringing in arbitrary style or aesthetics to the building; things are grown from within with this design model. They become timeless because you can't take anything away. They are there for a reason and it's crafted and composed

in a way that is compelling, formally and aesthetically.

I think that is our challenge now, to take all the systems and competing demands and weave them together in a way that is compelling. Now that we have these red lists, all our other projects benefit, and hopefully as people become more aware of toxicity, for instance, the industry responds. The city has been a good partner, and has implemented a program to find errors in the building code that are limiting people's ability to design ultra sustainable or Living Building Challenge projects. For instance, you can build 10 feet higher if you show improvement in natural daylight.

The project was under constant value engineering. Anything that was not contributing to the goal of the Living Building Challenge was out, there's nothing extra on the building. We had a bunch of balconies and complicated massing diagrams that went away. I can say with a reasonable degree of comfort, that there is nothing on this project that does not have to be there. It was liberating in a way to have those kinds of restraints. We're not changing a lot of the core modernist principles, but we're adding the lens of looking at everything with efficiency and resource use.

We think this project is the future of design trends, and it has changed the way we work in this office. Everyone becomes more aware of the cost of energy, operations, maintenance, and buildings that last longer. People are willing to spend more on the front-end to get a project that is going to reduce its liabilities over the long-term. Something like only 20% of the capital costs of the building over its lifespan of say 50 to 60 years is in the construction of it, so if you invest at the beginning, you save over the long run. 🌁

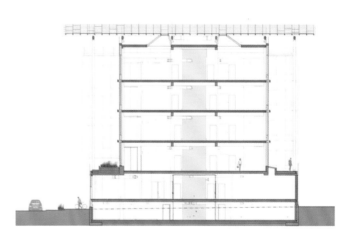

ARCHITECT
PERKINS + WILL
VANCOUVER, CANADA
2011
1,765 SQUARE METERS
LIVING BUILDING CHALLENGE
LEED PLATNIUM

[VANDUSEN BOTANICAL
GARDEN VISITOR CENTRE]

The VanDusen Botanical Garden is in Vancouver's Shaugh-nessy neighborhood and is a premier 55-acre urban garden in the temperate wet climate of the northwest. Completed in 2011, the Visitor Centre has achieved LEED Platinum and Living Building Challenge certification.

Spearheaded by Peter Busby, the new center is a diligent ex-ploration of the connectivity between the natural and built environments. The project's prominent curling vegetated roof, made with 71 custom roof panels, each comprised of 100 uniquely curved glulams, is an abstraction of a 1928 pho-tograph of an orchid by Karl Blossfeldt. Using nature as a guide, timber and rammed earth comprise a majority of the building fabric, maintaining the adherence to a strict materi-als sourcing radius. Crowned by an oculus in the center foyer the gesture catalyzes natural light and breezes to their fullest benefit. Net zero energy and onsite water capture and recla-mation help close the resource loops.

The Centre is a touchstone to the natural world and acts as an antidote to Vancouver's bustling and increasingly vertical grid, creating linkages for the city's inhabitants to the complex and diverse group of natural elements and species native to Brit-ish Columbia. The timber-supported vegetated roof acts as an elevated biophilic topography, maintaining the garden's rich biodiversity above the program of human activity.

PETER BUSBY

Cascadia in particular, and the West Coast in general, has attracted people with more environmental instincts. If you want to work for money, you go to Toronto. If you want a lifestyle that has environmental components to it such as skiing, sailing, hiking, clean air, fewer cars in your life, you head to Vancouver, Seattle, to Portland, for sure. I am learning that there is a big part of San Francisco that has similar interests. Environmental aspects of life are more real here.

Regenerative is about looking at ourselves as part of nature so that everything we do, for example, designing a building for a city, should regenerate nature. It should be seen as part of the natural system, whether it's water or waste or energy or materials. With the VanDusen Botanical Garden Visitors Centre we were trying to adhere to as many petals in the Living Building Challenge as we could, and obviously, local materials are one. We don't drive the design by LEED Platinum, we just work from the ground up. The project was about the botanical garden and trying to find something that was as natural as possible that referred to nature in materiality, and for what it did for nature in terms of being regenerative. And obviously if it's in nature it needs to feel natural, so wood and rammed earth became quite obvious.

Sustainable building, like LEED, is about doing less bad. You get to the point at the Living Building Challenge where you really are truly sustainable. You are having negligible impact on energy demand or waste creation. Then what about moving beyond that? What about buildings that actually finish up with more biomass on the site than what was there before harvest

and add things? In VanDusen, human waste that's created there, blackwater or whatever, is treated onsite and the water is reused. It is nutrient rich so it helps the plants and the sludge is composted and used in the garden. The roof is covered with various types of plants that were selected to support biological communities of butterflies, critters, and bugs. The roof connects with the ground so that the critters can get up on the roof. There is a deliberate attempt to make nature better as a result of the presence of the building and the human use of it. We wanted the indoor-outdoor spaces to blend together, and we wanted views of the lake and the flowers and the sunset. We wanted people to enjoy the inside-outside relationship of the building.

There is a very beautiful native orchid in British Columbia in the forests, and we took the form from that for the building. We extracted it. There is a series of leaves, if you will, that radiate from a central solar chimney and they are deliberately shaped to create an image of fitting into nature. It is an abstraction of a building as a natural form. For me, that was a first.

Because of its complexity, we wanted to pre-fab it. We wanted to make it in a factory on the floor. Wood is a natural material for that because there are lots of carpenters around who know how to create more complex shapes and structures. The glulams are the main members, but the secondary members are a laminated 2x4 structure that holds the glulams together. Those two main components form the panels of the roof. Those panels were pre-fabricated, fitted with everything including acoustic mat, electrical wires, lights, and a roofing membrane on top. It was shipped to the

site like that, fully complete, so they were just lifted off the truck and dropped onto vertical steel posts or wood posts, and they were installed in literally 20 minutes per panel. It rains a lot in Vancouver, of course, so a peal and stick panel came in a kind of envelope with an overlapping edge. So, as soon as a panel was in place, we could flip an overlapping piece of laminate to the adjacent piece of roof that was already there. It became watertight within 20 minutes of coming to the site, preserving the wood.

The central oculus is a sheet of thick, solid aluminum, and the purpose of that oculus is to be a heat sink. It is designed to catch the sunlight and get hot. In getting hot, it heats up the air around it and goes out through the top of the solar chimney. The hotter it gets, the more air that moves through the pipe. So, it is shaped to respond to the altitude and to the azimuth of the sun. It is not even symmetrical because you want more in the afternoon and the evening than you do in the morning. The relationship between sun path and performance needs for ventilation is embedded in the design and passive performance of it.

In your career as an architect, you start off with all rectangular buildings because clients don't have any money and stay with that or you blow the budget. And later on you can start experimenting with more radical shapes when there are a few more bucks around. I did a semi-circular university building, Nicola Valley Institute of Technology, all in wood and concrete 15 years ago. It was the first use of vertical wood to support concrete floors in North America. Then obviously with the development of Rhino software, we are able to model 3D shapes more easily. Rhino was a liberating tool for architects, allowing us to conceive of things in three dimensions much more readily, and draw them.

I try to make the buildings look like a result of the environmental design as much as the use and occupancy of the building. So, all four elevations are different because they are doing different things, the wind or the sun, something like that. They also may be different for functional needs. This is the entrance side, that is the poolside, or something. The fabric of the building should respond to environmental criteria as much as anything.

The relationship to nature is much more than just using wood in a building. It is a commitment to try to find an architecture that is connected to nature. We started working with wood 15 plus years ago, and gradually we have been exploding all the myths about it's not durable, or it requires more maintenance, or it's a fire problem. Gradually, we have exposed and explored those issues and convinced our clients, and more and more building types, that it is a great material. And from an environment

point of view, of course, the fact that you are sequestering carbon at the tune of 66% of the weight of the building is a really positive story. It is a net positive from a carbon point of view in its fabric, not just in its operation. Certainly, many people have picked up on that. When it was finished, the calculations showed there were 600 tons of carbon sequestered in the wood of the building, and 525 tons in all the other things in the building like the carpets, the windows, the aluminum, so it is a net carbon positive story.

Carbon is still the major global environmental issue. We still have to deal with that, and by and large as a community we are not. Over the life of the building there's much more carbon involved in the operation of the building than there is in the fabrication. But there are still significant amounts of carbon involved in the fabrication. Don't forget, the construction materials' industry is the largest industry in North America. Far and away there is more money spent on producing stuff for building than anything else. We can find low carbon solutions to get the industry to become

less carbon intensive, whether that's the transportation or the finish, or fabrication method. If you compare concrete or steel to wood in terms of carbon, the issues are hugely different. Cement is the number one source of carbon in our atmosphere from a single source. Eight percent (8%) of the carbon in our atmosphere comes from cement production. It is stunning, when you think of it.

Architects are not into the carbon impact of materials yet, but they will be. There will be a point in time when they will have to say, our building is net zero but also, what is the carbon footprint of the fabric of the building? That leads you directly to lower impact solutions such as rammed earth, or wood, or stone, things that come from nature. Even brick is good. I am looking into doing a hospital in wood, trying to convince clients to do high-rise office buildings in wood, you know? Bite the bullet, I think it can be done.

We built big wood buildings in the past. All the big warehouses that were built in the 1800s across North America were all built

Nic Lehoux

Nic Lehoux

in wood. There were big trees in those days and you just cut it down, milled it to shape, and stuck it up. Go to any old part of any old city in North America and the biggest oldest buildings usually have brick load-bearing perimeter walls and wood structure inside. Laminated wood structures are durable. These are the warehouses that are now cool condos in older parts of cities. They survived 100 years for various purposes and now they are being reclaimed as interesting loft apartments and those kinds of things. It's durable, it's flexible, requires little or no maintenance.

One of our first buildings in wood was the Brentwood SkyTrain Station in Vancouver. It is 15 years old now and if you go there now, today, just like classic public infrastructure gets little or no maintenance, the steel paint is peeling, but the wood looks just as good as the day we finished it. People always say we can't use wood because it requires more maintenance, well there's a building that's had no maintenance for 15 years and the part that looks good is the wood, because it doesn't need repainting.

Wood construction employs trades that elevate the craft of building. If you pre-fabricate in a factory, you are going to spend more time making the artifact beautiful because the labor is more efficient. Builders are happier; they are able to be more precise and put things together more carefully. The artifice that comes out of it doesn't need to be covered up. When you work with steel or concrete, or something, at the end of the day it all gets covered up because it doesn't look that good. Unless you are really fussy about the forms or other types of very expensive efforts in making the concrete look good, you end up covering it up. With wood, you don't have to do that. If it is put together nicely, you can just reveal it and people like it. People like working in environments that have wooden ceilings because it is softer, it is more humane, and it is less institutional. You also don't have to put stuff up that you question where it was made or what factory it came out of, what was the process and what were the chemicals in it? Everybody knows what's in a piece of wood and what goes on top of it.

It has been a process of education and it has been endless, completely endless my entire career. First of all, just convincing the clients that they need an environmental approach, and convincing the people who work in them, that they should be more environmental and that they should care about this building is difficult. The more green buildings we get built, the more people will see them and enjoy them, feel healthier in them, and then there will be more and more of them. Health issues are coming to the forefront. You know, we spend most of our lives in buildings and many of them are poisoning us.

It's not rocket science. There is nothing I am doing that was not well-known to the Victorians. They didn't have air conditioning. They didn't have electric lighting. They didn't have all the things that we have that consume energy. They had to have ceiling fans and windows that opened at the bottom and at the top of the wall to let out the hot air. They had to create E-shaped and courtyard buildings so that daylight would get to 100% of the building. None of the stuff I am doing is new. I don't rely on technology; it's about understanding the natural process. 🙶

Nic Lehoux

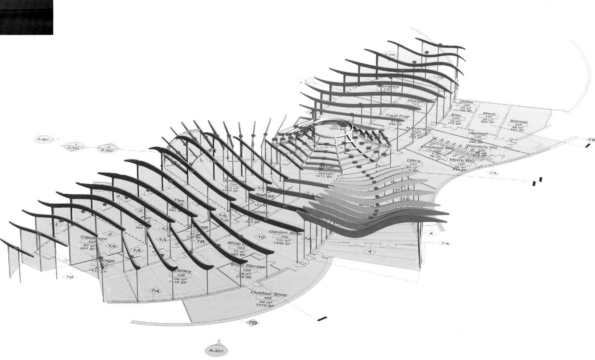

JAPAN

CONDENSES]

They are called *kyosho jutaku*, these tiny Japanese homes which seem to captivate the world. Perhaps it is their excessive constraints or the endlessly clever ways architects imagine them both inside and out. The reason for this rich miniaturized building movement is both inspirational and surprisingly complex. It is a blend of a critical density, advanced space making formulated from traditional architecture, an appetite for inventiveness, and a peculiar property market with few building codes. Little supply and high demand for land has left few affordable plots left to build on, provoking would-be home owners to sink their investment into a high design but diminutive homesteads.

With walls relatively under-insulated to secure every fraction of a meter of living space, the houses are anything but energy efficient. A new house may have practically no insulation but the toilet seat is always heated. Yet a Japanese home on average uses 45% less energy than an American one due to the occupants' higher tolerance for discomfort, localized space heating and cooling, and, of course, a much smaller occupied space to condition. Now ubiquitous here, mini-split systems and on-demand water heaters are sought out for energy and space savings.

To understand how these homes work you have to step back and consider how a city like Tokyo is stubbornly immense. If thought of as a single article, the city is easily the largest and most complex thing ever built by humans. This outcome was not necessarily planned, but the result of very loose land use and construction codes and high demand for an urban lifestyle. Waves of post-war construction amplify the consecutive period's social priorities, which typically veer to a more Western-influenced building palette. Neighborhoods grow because a liberal land use code allows building programs to switch as the owner deems. This allows a rapid capacity of small commercial growth and resulting penetration of services into neighborhoods. While

immense apartments are everywhere, many still feel that a single-family home is the ideal living condition. Thus, small neighborhoods, sometimes best accessible by a path, line the large commercial districts and spread out beyond the horizon in almost any given direction.

By embracing an extended living space into the public realm, the need for private space is generously reduced. This phenomenon is a central tenet of many cities worldwide, but a modest need for personal environmental penetralia changes how design can function. Outwardly, the reduced footprint of individual homes allows for a greater resource of street-side amenities to develop. Tokyo is basically a vast collection of villages where you have everything you need in perhaps a 10 minute walk. Parks become backyards, restaurants are living rooms, and almost any private amenity is offered street side, famously embodied by the tiny capsule hotels for businessmen who do not have time to go home at night. The density of pedestrian use also adds a valuable layer of security as more eyes are on the street.

This greater-built environment subsidizes the privately-designed environment, allowing a family to live with less space but enjoy a contemporary lifestyle. A home does not need a garage when a car share is on the corner, and a train station is a short walk or bike ride away. A dining space becomes a living space when eating out is the best way to gather with friends and family. This fluid connection between the public and private is a powerful, unspoken design element core to a successful urban habitat.

Since privacy has not historically been a design priority in Japan, a home's interior is given great freedom to explore space making. By opening up the small volumes, architects can incorporate ingenious ways to design interiors visually, functionally, and psychologically larger than they would seem capable of. The egress from floor to floor becomes the light shaft, a vanishing point, space delineation, and an aural connection in one gesture. Daylight in itself, a mastered form in traditional Japanese architecture, creates interest in the volume. A single shaft of sunlight can penetrate though an entire living space, thus adding valuable depth. Junichi Sampei's House Tokyo draws in the light from above through elegant glass floors, while Cell Brick by Yasuhiro Yamashita stretches the walls both toward and away from the viewer with a grid of daylight. Negative space and transparency also play significant roles. The illusion of depth is mesmerizing and deeply practical. Perhaps the most provocative tool is the use of valuable space for something other than living, like a small garden in the middle of a house, or formal transition space, which has less utility than its proportion would suggest.

These devices of space making are the progeny of hundreds of years of architecture refinement. Traditional spaces largely preserved in more rural settings have largely been erased in the urbanization of post-war Japan. The cleansed palette was filled with Western forms, hitting a peak during the property bubble in the 1980s. Now, reinterpretations of the elusive Japaneseness with a contemporary lens are refining the grace of condensed space making. The way to unravel this connection with the past is by seeing it as temporal architecture.

The condensed houses of modern Japan are a vital link to the contemplative traditions of centuries earlier. Humble materials, space transitions, infusion of natural elements, light, and, most uniquely, designing for time are hallmarks. With the addition of time as a constituent in design, the program becomes much more fluid. Certainly a room's use can change over the course of a day. A traditional single-room home, whose layout was based on tatami mats roughly the size of a person lying down, would often have a core living space using the fusuma, or sliding walls, and translucent paper shoji screens

to partition the interior for various functions. A living space can convert quickly to a sleeping area with mattresses easily removed from a cabinet and placed next to the cooking fire for warmth. In summer, the residents would gravitate to the veranda where nights are cool. In the Small House the occupants do this vertically, to the upper floor above the kitchen in winter and cooler subterranean room in summer. PACO House fully embraces the principle of changing up the space rather than moving to a new program. Renovation Matsugaya uses light diffused in layers with floor-lit wall curtains to evoke the effect of shoji rooms from 500 years ago. The resulting subtle layers make the simplest of boxes an enriched interior. As space condenses, time dilates. Rooms no longer have need for Western labels, but function depending on user needs. The transformation of micro-environments is a direct translation of traditional homes by way of use, even if its form is utterly contemporary.

Looking forward, these designs are an authoritative vision of small-scale habitation for a world population becoming intensely urbanized. They create mindful relief from the chaos of the city street as the designation of home is materialized by gentle spaces.

One lasting and unique feature of living in a tiny space is that it may seem difficult to imagine not having the room to enjoy things to purchase and use. Without extra space, shopping for items quickly becomes a satiated activity. When I visited a high-end department store in the very busy Shinjuku District, I noticed that all of the action was in the basement where the consumables were. The floor was thick with shoppers waiting to sample and purchase a considerable assortment of refined delicatessen items, teas, and desserts. The floors above, full of household goods and knickknacks, were practically empty. Income is spent on the consumption of experiences rather than objects, a fascinating break from the Western model of consumerism.

ARCHITECT
SCHEMATA ARCHITECTS
ANYWHERE
2009
27 CUBIC METERS

[PACO HOUSE]

A residence this small is no longer a house but too large to be considered furniture. The intention is fully practical by condensing function to elements. It is small enough to be carried to a location—urban, industrial, natural—and support one person's need as a full-service shelter.

At 27 cubic meters, 3 meters to a side, the design relies on portative elements. The system is evocative of traditional Japanese rooms, which could transform through the day from a sleeping space to a kitchen to a living space. The insight with PACO is to push a transformative space to its logical conclusion. The shower and toilet are one. A table pops out of the floor and, with a simple 90-degree rotation, elevates to allow the user to place their legs underneath. A sleeping space is tucked below or in a hammock. Weather permitting, the roof hydraulically opens to provide an uninhibited view of the sky. The reality is that few would be willing to live in, much less stay in, such a small space, but stripping a living built environment to its essence is a powerful exercise in disbanding assumptions.

JO NAGASAKA

“ It is very much like the Kiosuku or small shops in Japanese train stations. They can take everything and move. In the city, PACO can be near the main house, it can be a guesthouse or for a tea ceremony. We only made two PACOs and none exist now. One was for exhibition, and the other one's owner had to move so it was removed. At that time, before the banking crisis, a developer wanted to use them for a hotel. Another company wanted to use it for advertising in Tokyo, but it is too expensive. From the outside it is hard to tell how it works, but the inside is enough for one person, and on a nice day it opens to the weather.

The original client was looking for something that was not a house and was not furniture, but the concept and the idea were my own. I have long wanted to have a roof open in a house, but houses are too big for that to work. So when the size was determined, I thought to myself that I would like to open the roof. It is something I had in mind for a long time.

We made the PACO here in our studio, and after the exhibition we designed it to come apart in pieces. Once the building was placed outside and sealed, it would be difficult to take it apart again. While the pieces are not very heavy, we did use a small crane to place it. It is possible to place it somewhere like a forest by carrying it in by hand. I think I would like to design something that is easier to place on the site and cheaper to construct. We have to make the idea simpler. What made this expensive is the small size because the small table and the kitchen were custom. I did worry about the roof becoming stuck as well because it was the first time hydraulic pistons were used like this.

It is a very small house. To make the table, you pull it out of the floor and turn it 90 degrees so it sits on the floor. The space underneath is now open for your legs. That space is used for three things. The toilet is the same; first there is a folding door in the floor. So, when you need to use the toilet you fold the door up, and for the shower you use the umbrella curtain and sit on the toilet. It is very Japanese, very small (laughs).

I didn't make it to be completely self-contained because it is such a small house. You will have to hook up power, water, and a sewer connection. Also, in the city you cannot separate the graywater from blackwater like you can in the country. We have a technique to recycle the rainwater for drinking, but the government will not allow us to use it.

Many people are interested in this house and have contacted us, but nothing has come of it. As I said, it is difficult to buy because it is expensive. We're not interested in letting somebody else take the plans to build one—we would like to build it ourselves. ”

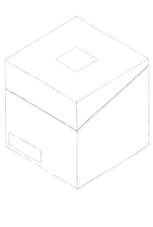

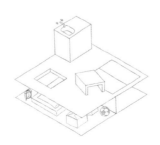

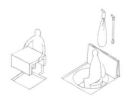

Takumi Ota

Takumi Ota

ARCHITECT
HIROYUKI UNEMORI
MEGURO, TOKYO, JAPAN
2010
67 SQUARE METERS

[SMALL HOUSE]

Designed for a young family on a very limited budget, Small House inverts the typical approach of developing a small urban Tokyo lot. The counter-intuitive design, in fact, uses less than half of the 34-square-meter lot, but, by cleverly interpreting the solar exposure code, the home is a full story taller than the neighbors. To further the usability of the stacked program, a unique post and floor suspension system allows for extremely thin floor plates. The walls are similarly complex in construction, utilizing cross bracing typically employed in bridges. All this is hidden behind a subtly simple exterior, punctuated by an elevated oversized door and window.

The use of the home is the clue as to how it is conceived. Rather than heating or cooling the entire space, the family has opted to move the sleeping area according to the season. This use evokes a traditional Japanese farmhouse. In the summer, in lieu of a veranda, the family sleeps in the lowest floor, which is half embedded in the ground. In winter, the family sleeps in the room directly above the kitchen for warmth. This is the traditional response when families would gather around the central hearth at night, only adapted for a verticalized volume.

Finally, by supplying two large openings to the street in the kitchen and dining space, the family can be connected to the neighborhood, and the neighborhood connected to them.

HIROYUKI UNEMORI

"This is my first project. The building footprint is half the size of the lot, which is six meters wide and five meters deep; while the house footprint is four meters by four meters. Because the house is so narrow I was able to make it taller. It is a very small space created for the clients' unique lifestyle.

It is on a typical narrow Japanese road, which is four meters wide and the house is set one meter in. In an ordinary house you would have the kitchen and living room on the same floor, and bedroom and bathroom on another floor, so the house takes up the entire lot. The client did not want this. My idea is to make the home four meters wide and nine meters tall, which is taller than the homes around it. One floor is one program. So you have four floors, a bedroom and entrance, dining room, spare room, and terrace room. To meet the height requirements is very difficult. You have to use a formula to make sure you do not block sunlight from the neighbors. Many homes built simply cut an angle on the north edge to meet the restriction. Because this house is so narrow we went taller and have the terrace on the south side. This also leaves room for bicycles on one side and a car on the other. The total floor space is only 60 meters.

The space is very small but it has big windows. There is a big window in the dining room that looks out to the street. There is a big door on the other side of the room that is two meters. So again, a very small floor, but there's a big door because the clients like the outdoors. Just above the dining room window is a covered window for the spare room.

I like a simple building, but also it is designed like this because the client has very little money. The materials are very simple and low cost. The interior is finished with lauan plywood on the floor and plaster board on the wall. I wanted to make the walls and floor very thin as well. The bathroom is on the top and opens out to a terrace. From the terrace you can see Tokyo Tower and Sky Tree. The basement floor is the bedroom, and the closet is underneath the entrance. There is also another toilet, since the home is for a small family.

The client previously lived in a very cool area of North Japan. In winter, the family sleeps in the upstairs room where it is warmer because it is above the kitchen. In the summer, the family sleeps in the lower bedroom partially underground where it is cooler. It is a lifestyle change from the neighboring houses where they use only one room to sleep in.

Typically, in a house like this, the floor is a shear component to keep the building from twisting in an earthquake. Instead, we use steel cross braces in the walls to keep the building rigid. This allowed me to design the floor for only the load it carries, which means it can be thinner. A post in the middle of the span supports the second floor, and a post attached to a large beam in the roof suspends the third floor. This leaves the dining room and kitchen open.

I did the engineering for the project, and it was very difficult. The cross bracing is offset—one side of the wall is open while the other is braced. Two heavy L brackets form the corners. The steel brace is shaped like a K where it comes to the frame, and the cross brace is then welded. The wall is like the frame on a bridge. In the end it becomes one piece that connects the window frames, the walls, and the fence on the top floor. So while the architecture is very simple, the design and construction is very complex. We even had to move the power pole in front of the house and replace it with a new one.

The large door in the dining room is two meters wide and three meters tall, with a very big screen door that slides in place. The door can swing open 550 millimeters, and is used in the summer to help cool the house and open it to the street. Because it is white it can reflect light into the space. Light can also come down the spiral staircase, and, because it is open, the family can communicate from the bottom floor to the top. The only real private room is the bathroom on the top floor. In the summer when the top floor is 33°C the bottom floor will be 26°C. Again, because of the temperature difference we do not use air conditioning, but naturally ventilate the interior so the client will sleep on the bottom floor in the summer and in winter sleep on the third floor.

Most buildings will have a small window to the street, which is something I do not understand. I like the house to open to the street, to have the occupants see those who walk by. In other houses there is no communication."

Ken Sasajima

Ken Sasajima

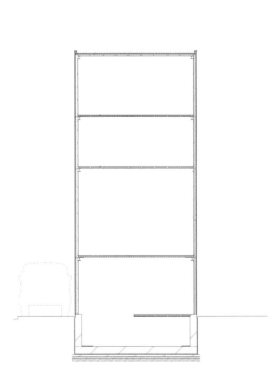

ARCHITECT
KUBOTA ARCHITECT ATELIER
YOKOSUKA, JAPAN
2007
114 SQUARE METERS

[T HOUSE]

Located a half hour south of Yokohama, facing Tokyo Bay, the austere concrete boxy form of T-House is set firmly, yet gently, into the hillside. From the street the form plays with the elements of water and air as a gesture to the bay seen though the split canopy. The lightness on top transforms on descent to a minimalist living space, completely open to the ocean view. The main floor shares a living space and separate small studio, both accessed by the sunken entrance. The lower floor shares the bedroom, bath, and a small outdoor room, giving access to a runway projected out from the home. The projection of the ramp acts as a more personal continuation of the play of elements experienced from the street and connects the home to the environment in a minimal and direct gesture.

The design is a clear resolution of the difficulties of building on hillside lots. The program is tucked into the hill, with each level stepping up in size as the incline retreats. Its street side "face" is the framed view beyond it, its footprint is a modest 86 square meters, and its presence is simply sculptural. While not large, the space instead uses the notion of establishing a sense of place through view. By replacing valuable usable area with a water element, the experience of place softens and ever so slightly defies gravity.

Kubota Architects

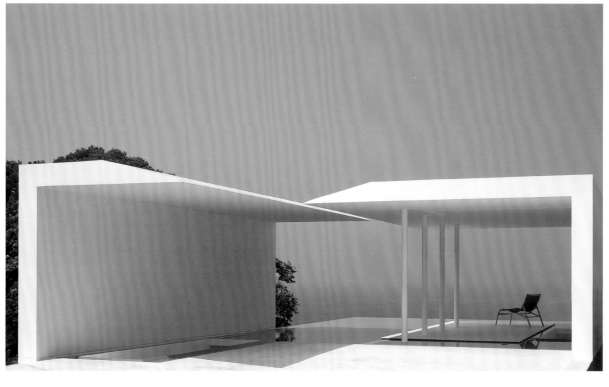

Anna Matsuoka

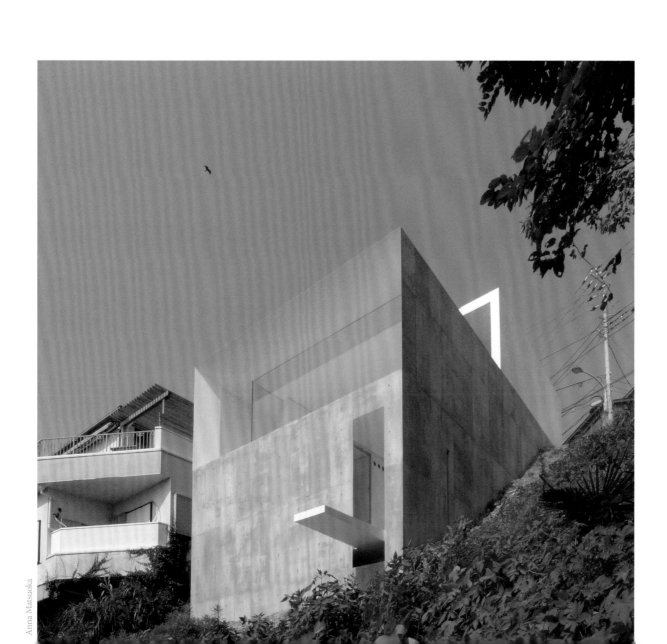

Anna Matsuoka

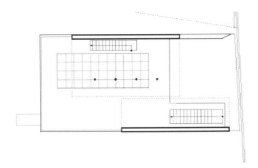

Kubota Architects

Kubota Architects

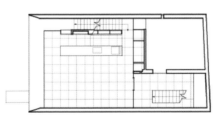

ARCHITECT
ATELIER TEKUTO
TOKYO, JAPAN
2004
85 SQUARE METERS

[CELL BRICK]

Cell Brick is located on a plot of land measuring 33 square meters and is no wider than the adjoining crosswalk. The restraint of size and location catalyzed a wholly unique design approach that is both modular but site specific. Steel boxes were bolted together in small sections off site and stacked like Tetris bricks to create an intricate and highly functional interior. The design serves multiple functions; structural, buildable, storage, privacy, light, and visually vigorous.

Creating capacity for storage is one of the most daunting challenges in a small home. By inverting the problem and making the structure the shelving, the design merges two separate design tasks.

The highly exposed corner lot does not detract from the home's ability to gather light but maintain a sense of privacy. The space's rigorous presence based on creating layers of scale draws the eye throughout. The dappled quality of fragmented light in the space is rigorous but natural. The architect speaks of the effect as being under a tree.

YASUHIRO YAMASHITA

"The stacked box exterior walls were realized because of three reasons. Our client requested enough storage space. Also the land price was very expensive in this area. We wanted to minimize the wall thickness in order to utilize the maximum space on this site. Finally, it was my personal interest and challenge to integrate daily life elements into the structural system.

When designing a living space, there are two general directions. One is to store all daily life goods in the closets to hide behind the covers. The other is to keep these goods visible and integrating them into architecture. I think that the latter requires strong architectural space. Such strong space unifies architecture and the daily life, and brings beautiful harmony.

This project combines opposing architectonics. There is the masonry structure which is the origin of the building technique and the skin structure which I have been trying on my projects. I wanted to innovate something that equips structure, function and heat environment altogether. A steel box is designed with the Japanese original module and it sizes 450mm×900mm. The boxes are piled up with openings that become windows. Considering the heating environment inside, the depth of a steel box was decided as 300mm that serves as brise-soleil. The given depth blocks out the summer sun light and pulls in the winter sun into the house. In addition, a heat resistance material, a special ceramic-infused coating which we have applied for the past Penguin House project, is put on the steel plate. This also helps to solve the heating problem.

For this project, I was especially concerned about and aiming to attain a 'special depth'. Because piled thin steel boxes cannot give depth to a space, I was thinking of putting parting strips and deck shelves (it also serves as an essential structural material) from the beginning. To avoid making a dull space, the interior wall is made like multiple layers and it gives a certain sense of depth. By inserting translucent and transparent glass and steel panels into openings between the boxes, the occupants can enjoy beautiful flickering light coming from the openings as if sitting under a tree. And when they put their personal belongings in the steel boxes, a 'life layer' is added and a layering process comes to the end.

This project is supported by the steel boxes only. A vertical load goes down through the edge of boxes like 'Ghost Leg' shape and a seismic force is supported by a row of backboards that becomes like a big wall. In order to pile up the boxes, detailed planning took place over the design, structure, and construction. At the same time, from the very beginning, cost and precision of building frame were crucial topics in the process. At first, we planned to assemble each boxe on site but the precision of construction, cost and time became problematic. And eventually, we decided to unitize boxes and fuse them with high-tension bolts previously at the factory. The size of each unit is decided to respond to the size of the truck. Because the frontal road of the site is too narrow for a large truck to pass, it is effective to adopt this stacking method of small components.

After the 2011 earthquake, I am focusing on using natural and locally-obtained materials of each region."

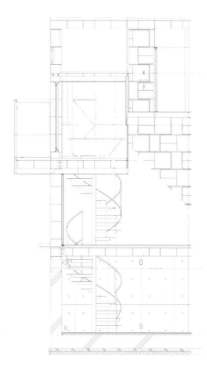

Makoto Yoshida

[JAPAN CONDENSES] Cell Brick

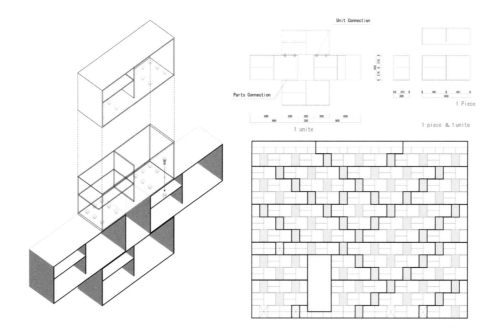

Unit Connection

Parts Connection

1 unite

1 Piece

1 piece & 1unite

Makoto Yoshida

[JAPAN CONDENSES] Cell Brick

ARCHITECT
TNA
TOKYO, JAPAN
2011
83 SQUARE METERS

[MIST HOUSE]

ARCHITECT
ARCHITECT LABEL XAIN
CHIBA PREFECTURE, TOKYO, JAPAN
2008
55 SQUARE METERS

[RENOVATION MATSUGAYA]

One of the most evocative elements of traditional Japanese architecture is the humble shoji screen. Using rice paper glued to a delicate wooden lattice to transform space is still practiced in contemporary life throughout the world. This manipulation of softening light is the core principle behind a gently renovated ground level work and living space in an unassuming urban building in west Tokyo. With only a large plate glass window and a solitary 55-square-meter room already plumbed, the architect uses a humble palette to give it layers of space.

The first measure is to raise the floor halfway into the volume to create the delineation of public and private. Delicate cloth screens line the sides, running on tracks inspired by hitofude-gaki calligraphy, meaning single stroke. Highlighted by light embedded in the floor, they delineate the space into three zones and compensate for the lack of natural light. The transformation is startling for the simplicity of the intervention.

SAMPEI JUNICHI

"This space was designed so the client can use it in many different ways, to inhabit as a living space or offices. This was my first renovation project, so it was a good opportunity for me to ask myself what it means to renovate. I typically design new houses, so I make the connection between raw land and architecture. But this project is very different for me because I am working with the existing conditions. I am glad to hear comments on how the project is very simple. The client is a designer who lives in Osaka, but when he works in Tokyo he stays here and uses the space as an office.

The curtain is the architecture. It becomes more difficult to see through the space when the curtains are pulled out. I put the most private spaces in the back, then semi-private, then the public space at the front.

Because in this project I could not control the sunlight, I had to introduce the light to make the space. Using the light below curtains created a visual depth to the space. Because I could not introduce light from outside, I still sought to create a natural light. I wanted to create a soft light like on an overcast day.

I used texture on every surface except the floor. The doors, the hardware, and even the air conditioning are textured and painted the same as the walls. I did this to match what was introduced with the existing finish. Twenty years ago I created a room where every product was the same color, so maybe that influenced me. I design every building as one I would also want to live in."

Koichi Torimura

Koichi Torimura

Koichi Torimura

Koichi Torimura

Koichi Torimura

ARCHITECT
ARCHITECT LABEL XAIN
MUSASHINO, TOKYO
2010
78 SQUARE METERS

[HOUSE TOKYO]

One of the most prized qualities of a small space is daylight, but it is also one of the most difficult to apply when building densely. House Tokyo masters light by letting it slip in from above, past the glazed deck and bath, through the suspended stair and glass floor, and onto the sunken living space. The bedroom is suspended away from the wall to allow perforated screened windows to dapple light from the sides. The open volume then allows them to mingle on the austere grey walls.

The occupants engage with a fully realized three-dimensional program. The interior is only 78 square meters in a footprint that completely fills the tiny corner lot. Yet the complexity of the volume created by the suspended rooms, fed by a meandering stair, creates an optical wealth of information. Coupled with raw materials like concrete and glass, the effect is a rich, layered living environment.

The exterior tells a very different story. The robust white treatment, tilted walls, and covered windows make the volume hard to read in both scale and purpose. Taking advantage of the corner lot, the house acts like a backdrop to the constant movement of people on the street. Their silhouettes cast on the wall like a spontaneous shadow theater. The exterior also adds a reprieve from the cluttered and dense neighborhood, and for the architect emphasizes the immediate built environment around the house. The building then becomes a contemplation on the reality of its surroundings.

SAMPEI JUNICHI

The site of the house is on a small piece of land that was connected to the house next to it. The original plot was small but was further divided in half. The smaller the lot, the cheaper it becomes because in Tokyo you can divide the land to ever smaller plots. In general, people around the world live in collective housing. However, the Japanese do not like to live in apartment blocks; they like to own their own homes. Now we cannot divide the land anymore.

For House Tokyo design was very important for the owners. They were interested in how to make such a small home very beautiful and livable. To start, the owner wanted a home made with concrete. The home is for a couple and child, and the grandparents live close by so the location is very important. The clients preferred concrete because they feel safer with that construction.

As you know, this building is very small and cannot open outwards, so it is important to bring daylight in from above. I wanted to make the biggest room on the ground floor and, for me, the home is one where I put different components in. In Tokyo you can see many buildings where the top is cut off at an angle to allow sun for the neighbors, but I did not want that. To achieve the setback I instead angled the walls, which maximized the ground floor size. Even though the house is on such a small plot of land, it is tall enough to feel open inside.

In the future, the small room suspended above the living space will be for the young daughter. Also above is the main bedroom and then a half level across is the bathroom. The bathroom was very important for the client because they wanted something like a spa. I made it feel like it was outside by visually connecting the bath to the roof patio; so, it is difficult to tell what is inside and what is outside, what is more public or private space.

The tall window to the street corner allows light but keeps the interior private. Inside you cannot see through the scrim, you can only see shadows as there are many people walking in the street, lots of cars and bikes. When you sit by the window you can only feel people passing by, even if they are just 50 centimeters away.

The complexity of the space is a result of the importance of getting the daylight into the home, so that the light can go anywhere inside. The walls can support all of the elevated spaces so there are no columns inside.

The home is less than 80 square meters, but I have done many projects of this size. It is quite normal for Japanese homes to be this small. The clients enjoy the space because even though it is so light filled it is still private and quiet. It is a space you can get very used to living in.

The neighbors often talk about the building.

They are very interested in knowing what kind of building it is because they did not think of it as a house. In Tokyo people often can visualize what is inside because of where appliances are, like the air conditioning for instance. But I wanted to design an abstract structure where it is hard to understand what is inside. The abstract architecture also provides privacy.

There are two reasons why it is named House Tokyo. The first is because the size is so typical of homes in Tokyo, and secondly, the house creates a space that emphasizes the buildings around it. This is achieved by both how abstract it is and by the whiteness, which creates the stark contrast in the neighborhood. It is this contrast that creates the emphasis on the surrounding homes. I design buildings to have a relationship with the surrounding buildings as well as the environment. For many of my projects I use the same material and paint the buildings white.

I have an obsession with materials. It is very typical for Japanese homes to use concrete for walls but to paint them to look like brick. In House Tokyo I prefer to keep the concrete untouched. The whole city of Tokyo is finished like a fake computer graphic design. It is up to many architects to find ways to approach this problem. My approach is to create calm spaces with a simple visual impact. 🙾

[GERMANY

[KUNSTMUSEUM RAVENSBURG]

MAINTAINS]

Walking though a Stuttgart neighborhood to visit UN Studio's wondrous metallic knot, the Mercedes-Benz Museum, I come across an otherwise rather ordinary building which catches my attention. It is a new three-story apartment with pale stucco and an innocuous entrance, but the windows sit deeper in its wall than a typical building and then there is something about how it was shaped. I approach the textured stucco skin wall to gave it a rap with my knuckles. Rather than receiving the expected thud, the resonance was is of a reverberation that you would get from a very tight drum. It is the sound of 250 millimeters of insulation exquisitely separating the inside from the outside, providing verity that this apartment is built based on Passive House principles.

This same result is confirmed at a massive Passive House development I visit on my way back from the Passivhaus Institut in Darmstat the next day. BahnStadt, named after its proximity to the train station in Heidelberg, is a dozen or so sizable mixed-use Passive House buildings, either freshly completed or in various stages of construction. It is the largest project of its kind in the world. Since it is dusk and the building crews are gone, I take the opportunity to slip into some of the projects still under construction.

Most of the apartment buildings are not much more than very well-adorned boxes, but what boxes. These constructions are singularly masters of controlling heat flow. Thick graphite embedded extruded polystyrene is being adhered to the concrete cores like giant play bricks. The windows and doors are feats of engineering with substantial frames for the three panes of glass, and tight fitting with triple seals and surrounding locking pins, all suspended from the raw concrete egress with thermal bridge free brackets. They are embedded in the deep walls and wrapped diligently with foam to minimize energy losses from the substantial frames, which

are already thermally optimized. Inside, the only signs of a climate system are little ducts running room to room that connect to the fresh air Heat Recovery Ventilator. That is a placid respite from the whirring and often overly complex technology that is stuffed behind the walls and ceilings of today's buildings.

This effort, based in Germany but gaining attention and credibility worldwide, is at the heart of the sea change in how we understand energy efficient buildings. The level of control of the elements is the key, and environmental building starts with a fundamental understanding of how environments actually influence buildings. The deeper intention of localizing our architecture is to maximize the inherent conditions of the site. These projects are based on a deep but accessible understanding of how we conserve and extract the energy we need from the immediate environment around us before we rely on outside, typically very dirty sources of energy. Showing great restraint, Passive House is the analysis and execution of the meticulous balance of heat losses to the exterior with heat gains from the sun, occupants, and electrical devices. The same works in reverse to keep heat out when needed.

The Germanic quality of intensely focusing on the core stringent efficiency goals has opened up a spectrum of new building typographies that excel in quality and energy miserliness. While the original super-insulated houses were developed in the 1980s in the upper Midwest of the US, the principles were refined and systemized by Bo Adamson and Dr. Wolfgang Feist in Europe. Dr. Feist went on to develop the system, first at the University of Darmstadt, and then founding the Passivhaus Institut to focus on research and the certification of buildings.

Rather than incrementally implementing changes to afford efficiency gains, as is typical in the conservative world of construction, the grassroots movement of Passivhaus has approached the consumption of energy from the opposite side of the spectrum. Design a building's shell that steeply reduces energy use to the point that its savings in ongoing operating costs justifies the added expense of the envelope over the life of the project. Create conditions where a minimal amount of technology is needed for the building to operate. That equation translates to 80% less than what typical new buildings use to heat and cool the interior. Keeping control of thermal losses and gains can be complex and stubbornly subtle, so a Passive House leaves little to chance. This discipline of maintaining has inspired entire industries. While becoming codified in some cities and regions, the standard has also pushed the agenda of very high performance far enough that many companies have noticed and supply products and services to meet the ever-growing demand.

The primary strategy is to use a few hard and fast but stringent energy thresholds: 15 kWh a year per square meter heating and cooling, 122 kWh yearly a square meter for all other energy loads and an air tightness of .60 air changes an hour at 50 pascals testing pressure. The system is non-prescriptive in that the designer can choose how they want to achieve the thresholds. It is the heating and cooling metric which has been the primary driver of the careful envelope design. This promise of a very high performance building comes with a steep learning curve, and even after thousands of certified projects across the world with some 50,000 built to or near the standard in Europe, the evolution of products and construction methods is constant. The greatest, or maybe only, leap of faith in Passive House is that by making it so rigorous, architects embraced the challenge rather than scoffing, creating buildings which perform to the theoretical

limits of building science by exploring the entire gamut of thermal performance.

The other key goal is comfort. I asked Dr. Benjamin Krick, head of component testing at PHI, to help me describe the meaning of comfort in Passive House. Surprisingly he did not have a suggestion. Explaining the metric to minimize the mean temperature gradient of internal surfaces to vastly improve comfort and over compensation in heating does not help. Think of being barefoot on a concrete floor in winter. Even a warm room will not make up for the discomfort from the lower extremities, so typically we will boost the heat to compensate. In Passive House a significant level of insulation is used to make those surfaces similar in temperature. The same principle applies to the windows. They are not designed to just save energy but reduce radiant heat loss from bare skin and provide another path to maintain thermal well-being. This is a situation few experience for any amount of time in a typical building, and for those in a Passive House it is almost purely experiential.

Arguably, from an energy perspective, no other system has come close to creating a platform that revitalizes the building science sector. Perhaps the ultimate nod is the codification of Passive House in many municipalities in Germany. The drive towards a principle rather than a technology has created two distinct but intertwined paths. The broad demand for innovation in products and systems has accelerated turnkey high-performance buildings by engaging the marketplace. This is in stark contrast to a general construction industry spoiled by incrementalism and generational change. Second, the mass adoption of the standard throughout Europe and worldwide demonstrates that community engagement and peer support for high performing buildings is a shared human value.

ARCHITECT
LEDERER + RAGNARSDOTTIR + OEI
RAVENSBURG, GERMANY
2013
25,000 SQUARE METERS
PASSIVHAUS CERTIFIED

[KUNSTMUSEUM RAVENSBURG]

The integration of a Passive House certified museum into the fabric of a medieval city challenges the identity of architecture by bridging 500 years of vernacular with a single gesture. The museum maintains the city's fabric with a nod in materiality and form, but resolutely avoids mimicry or nostalgia. If you quickly walked passed it you may not even recognize it is of our era. The barrel vault roof relief and rich, historical brickwork allow the mass to slip into the old, dense neighborhood with only a whisper and wink of the contemporary on the outside.

Pass the first-of-its-kind revolving door and you'll find a familiar 21st-century interior. Crisp white rooms host 20th-century Expressionism and Contemporary art in a nearly hermetically sealed container. Three floors for display and a basement archive make for a tidy program, one that does not attempt to distract from the contents. The journey to the top is where the design's coup d'état occurs. The tapering brick vault ceiling pulls you out of the airy space and plants you back into the old town.

The museum's effort not only bridges the past with the present, but stretches into the future by embracing the challenging energy standard of Passivhaus which originated only 350 km north in Darmstadt. By incorporating extremely low energy use, integrating the tried and true use of thermal mass with exhaustive insulation, the museum stretches the possibilities of inferred vernacularism comfortably into our contemporary understanding of high-performance building. In a stroke the museum maintains the fabric of the town while maintaining an interior energy flow, a kind of radical conservatism.

ARNO LEDERER

The idea for building to Passivhaus standards came from the investor. He asked us if this would be a good idea because there are not many museums in Europe that are Passivhaus certified. We wanted to make it an experiment, to see if this works or if it does not work. At first we hesitated because we had no windows in the museum. Normally you need to have windows to get energy from the sun. So we tried to make a Passivhaus without windows, which is unusual and a little bit complicated. We did a school building as Passivhaus and it had a lot of windows to the south, so we could earn a little bit of energy from the sun. Because the museum is so small, we wanted to have closed rooms. The pictures do not need any daylight, so we maintained closed walls without windows in the galleries. It seemed at first to be counterproductive to the idea of Passivhaus.

For a long time we tried to make buildings with a lot of mass, like an old steamboat that takes a long time to stop. So if you have a very heavy building, like the old buildings, it takes a long time to get cold, or in the summer to get warm. So our idea was to make a very heavy building, which reacts very slowly to different climates. We have used this type of building for some 20 to 30 years, and now the investor came and asked if we can combine that with Passivhaus. We tried it and it worked.

We did try to incorporate Passivhaus in an earlier museum in Frankfurt because all buildings are going to be Passivhaus there, but it was too complicated. So we started again in Ravensburg and solved the problem, which was very technical. For instance, because the insulation was so thick, we needed unusual anchors to hold the brick veneer. There was no product on the market because this is not normal construction for Passivhauses. There are other things that normally do not work with Passive House, like the revolving door at the entrance. This was very complicated to design, it was like getting a PhD. Normally you would have two doors and an airlock, but if you make this in such a small building you need four meters to make it work. If both doors are open when a group enters then the airlock does not work. We thought it would be better to make this revolving door to save space. The manufacturer of the door designed it with the help of the Passivhaus Institut, the architect, and the developer. It was a long process, about two months, to design and discuss how the door would work. Because half is outside and the other half is inside, it needs to have a thermal break in the middle. At the point where the door revolves you cannot divide it, this is the weak point. You come to problems that seem very easy to resolve, but when you're working on it, it becomes very complicated. All these little things which

you do not think of before, you say, "Ahhh, it's no problem," then you come to it and you have to think about it.

In Germany, architects are trained in construction at the university, it is a main part of our education. Normally we do everything from the designing to the surveying, which is typical for German architects. So we have to know a lot about these technical things and work with the construction details. I think that is why Passivhaus is successful in Germany because these two things come together. In the German-speaking countries like Switzerland and Austria, there are a lot of experiments with Passivhaus. Passivhaus does feel like taking a risk, but taking a risk is normal in architecture because you have to risk something.

I think the developer values the marketing and the contractor can claim they made the first museum in Passivhaus. It's a little bit like the auto industry where if they are in front of the technical process they can sell cars. With buildings there seems to be a similar interest to make it technically perfect, save energy, and if we can do this then there is a market. For me, I know this building saves a lot of energy and that is what counts.

The lighting is all LED, and because we did not like off-the-shelf lamps we combined it with the construction. In the classroom

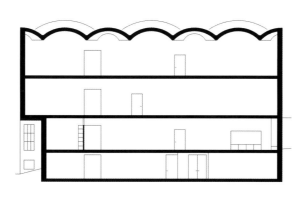

we designed the lamps because this is something we also like to do. We put a lot of effort into the staircases. The emergency exit is like underwear; we like to have very nice underwear also.

Every person who comes into the building is like a little oven, and the museum expected to have 25,000 visitors in one year, but in the first two months 20,000 people came. This was a little bit of problem because they were all heating the building too much. This is also a problem in general with Passivhaus because you have to plan for how many people will be in the space. There is a radiant cooling system in the concrete ceiling and very slow cooling is happening with the fresh air system. The ducts are behind the lights in the ceilings and walls. We didn't want to show how the system works. To control humidity, we have a "big machine in the cellar" (laughs) and I

don't know how it works. It was a problem for engineers to solve because it's too complicated for architects.

Our approach to the design was based on two things. We think it is better not to think in terms of times, only to make a good building. Ravensburg is a very nice town and we were allowed to contribute to it. It is like we started with a cake and we put something on the cake. Our building is a continuation of the town. And the second idea is using old materials. Until the 20th century, people used old buildings to build new buildings, starting with the Greeks then Romans, and into the Middle Ages, and even after the Second World War people built with the materials from the ruins. This is one aspect in which we are very interested in, that's why we used these old bricks. The bricks came from Cologne. We have a customer there who

knows we like old materials and he bought them for us. We used normal construction, construction that existed 120 years ago.

When you first see the building we hope the first impression is that it's very normal, very common. It starts with a second look, where you may think to yourself, "Oh there's something funny." How people come through the town to the building at first is very important. There is a little courtyard between the street and the building. It's good to have such a courtyard because it is a little more silent than on the street, people can gather before they go into the building. When you see the profile from the outside you want to go inside to see more of it. Again, it is old construction, very handcrafted. It's not industrial and it works well with the old buildings around it, which are handcrafted. **"**

Roland Halbe

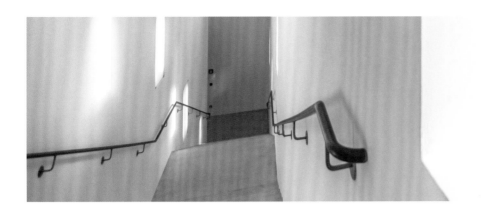

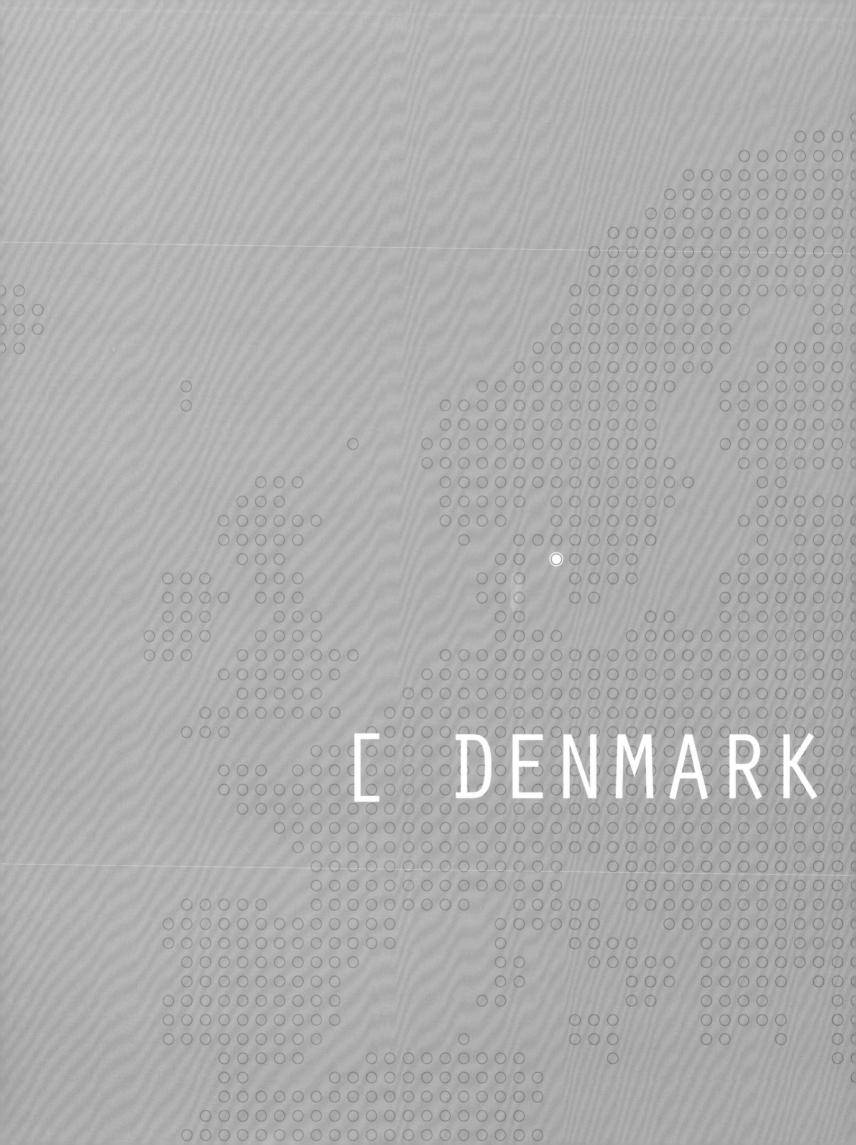

[DENMARK

[8 TALLET]

PLAYS]

By the 1960s, Denmark's growth as a modern state took on many of the characteristics of the other Western nations. Copenhagen was festooned with cars and was becoming ringed with suburbia. Then it took a left turn. After an oil crisis and botched proposals to link the city with large-scale road projects that would swallow the open space, folks voted with their pedals. Bicycles had been around for a long time, of course, but as the city needed to develop a more comprehensive transportation network, the culture of riding was introduced as a design element. Now 50% of all residents use a bike for their daily commute. This is just the start of a much more interesting movement in the great old city which is having a hard time growing up and taking itself too seriously.

Consider that the social experiment of Christiana, a neo-anarchist community, shares the same city that invented the amusement park. Not the famous Tivoli Gardens, which is in the town center, but Dyrehavsbakken, which was established in the late 1500s just north. An active

street life and a socially progressive culture and counterculture keep the metropolitan fresh. So, from a design perspective, it is a good place for experimentation. The architecture firm MLRP got in the act with their Mirror House, a pavilion sided with a giant funhouse mirror. 3XN decided that the city needed the most leaning towers in the world with the Bella Sky Hotel.

The Danish take the proverb "half the fun is getting there" very seriously. There is Dissing+Weitling's Cykelslangen or The Bicycle Snake, a sinuous elevated bike path along the river. The Green Way is an LED-indicated bike route which helps riders time the lights through the city. Then the Cycle Superhighway system links the entire region safely and quickly by bike. The bike infrastructure is thriving not just for convenience but also because people genuinely enjoy taking a bike ride as a part of their daily work and social life. The city is being designed so people have a good time as they transverse it, while also eliminating their carbon footprint.

The idea of traversing is one of the distinguishing marks of Denmark's prodigious architecture firm Bjarke Ingels Group (BIG). They cannot help but have people jump, walk, scoot, climb, bike, and ski on their creations. Their work seems to be as much about movement as it is monument, starting with their first large commission, a swimming pavilion in Copenhagen Harbor.

Movement and architecture can go very well together. Salted with a strong sense of environmental and cultural values, you have the backdrop for 8 Tallet (8 House), which at 61,000 square meters is Copenhagen's largest building. The mixed-use project is one of BIG's most clairvoyant ideas because it is a fully realized reinterpretation of an old city block. All the elements are there; a commercial street front, offices in the back, mixed-income living topped with sun-filled penthouses facing the windswept Kalvebod Faelled plains to the south.

But the design twist is not its slender midsection comprising the "8" which is the social hub of the project. It is the vertical-ization of the winding sidewalk, which meets every staggered floor in the building and goes down the side as a massive stair-case next to the vegetated roof. The project epitomizes BIG's tendency to create mass and then let people crawl all over it. The building is fun because it is all about going through it. You cannot help but want to take a bike ride down...

ARCHITECT

BIG

ØRESTAD, COPENHAGEN, DENMARK

2010

62,000 SQUARE METERS

[8 TALLET]

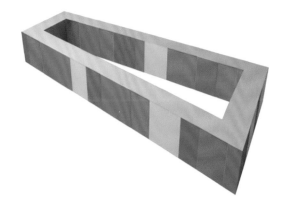

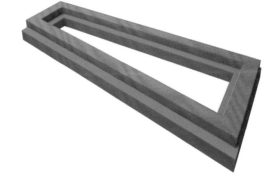

SPAIN

[BIBLIOTECA DE CAN LLAURADOR]

[NEW CITY HALL ARCHIDONA]

[FERRER RESEARCH & DEVELOPMENT CENTER]

[INSTITUTE OF NEUROSCIENCES OF CASTILLA Y LEÓN]

[COMISARIA FUENCARRAL]

[E8 BUILDING]

[BASQUE HEALTH DEPARTMENT HEADQUARTERS]

WRAPS]

In a landscape blessed with and challenged by the sun, and witness to countless generations of settlements often built on the ruins of eras before, a culture that embraces the contemporary has made its mark. Spain is now saturated with solar and wind installations, high speed train networks lacing the countryside, and one of the best road networks I have ever used, connecting the ancient cities and villages. But a construction boom and bust has laid bare the realities of growth by larding up the built environment with mediocre and ostentatious buildings.

One of the tragic trends in larger-scale architecture, which has been embraced by the green building movement, is the reliance of technologies to overcome the inherent shortcomings of the building. This practice began by separating the load-bearing structure from the building fabric and erecting lightweight, typically glass, curtain walls. The other vital component was the widespread adoption of air conditioning, which meant that these new lightweight, therefore cheaper, buildings could be built anywhere to a standard criteria. The fact that they were multiple times less energy efficient than mass construction in warm regions was, at best, a secondary thought. Floor plates grew ever wider as well, relying on artificial light to the point where it did not matter if it was day or night, and creating places that function the opposite of the modernist principle of expansive, naturally lit environments. Glass-clad buildings are now the

universal design worldwide, yet they are the single worst form in terms of energy use. Solar and internal heat gains mean a constant demand for air conditioning to make them habitable, even in cold climates. Then at night they bleed energy outwards.

Moving forward, commercial architecture needs to maintain the benefits of a system which is lightweight, highly adaptable, naturally lit, and reevaluates energy needs, all the while exploring dynamic forms and functions. The answer is in the skin. By wrapping buildings architects have a dynamic tool to express design through function. The use of brise-soleils, derived from French for "sun breaker," creates a vital control layer and architectural tool for solar radiation control. Like the separation of the structure from the skin, the evolution of high-performance building is the separation of the solar control from the environmental boundary. It can take the form of glass, wood, perforated or plate steel, wire, block, plants. The list is only the limits of our invention.

Solar control may seem straightforward, like putting on a baseball cap and sunglasses, but its nuances are many. The first question is always where is the sun. In the morning, the eastward face of a building causes glare. In mid-day it is easier to protect from the high sun, and bringing in controlled daylight creates many design possibilities. A western orientation is the most problematic because the built-up heat of the day and low angle of sunlight can cause havoc with interior comfort, but as Ramón Fernández-Alonso notes it is also the most beautiful light to work with. Perhaps this is why Spanish architecture in particular is so well-versed in solar control. In a place of sun, these buildings navigate light like a mariner crosses the sea. Sunlight is dynamic and subtle, harsh and elegant, but most important, it is respected. It is the originator for the sense of space. It can create or overwhelm with the smallest of design gestures. It can save energy like no other single element, or take the most energy to vanquish its influence.

Solar control is also about coaxing gentle daylight deep into a space. These are the real solar-powered buildings. They use raw light and sculpt it for our eyes. This means reducing glare, introducing light from overhead, reflecting light, providing access to it from anywhere in the building. This is in all the design textbooks, but in practice is as much intuitive as it is technical. Rarely at any of the six projects I visited did I see an artificial light on during the day. This practice is completely out of the norm for commercial buildings. Lighting is one of the top three electrical loads in a building, depending on use. And because these projects tend not to overheat, they do not feel overly chilled or drafty as do so many modern buildings which are obligated to rely heavily on HVAC.

After all the technical aspirations are resolved, the real fun begins. Wrapping creates an unambivalent architectural presence. Coll-Barreu Arquitectos takes the second skin and fragments it. By using the reflected elements of the surroundings, their buildings become an observation on the nature of the space told through light. The effect is stunning; you can lose yourself witnessing them as an installation. Voluar's formal screens wrapping a police station allow the building to metamorphose through the day, either reflecting blues, silvers, and grays of ambient daylight, or disappearing in the evening hours to divulge the inner working of the police force. McDonough + Partners turns each side of the building into a micro-environment, which enriches the greater environment. Berta Barrio's library has aggressive light shelves that not only protect occupants from morning glare, but from the exterior they are abstract references to bookshelves, and from inside they help soften the space, providing as much a psychological tool as technical.

The expressive nature of wrapping is an antidote to shape making for its own sake. The formulation of these projects is in the service to the sun, which by nature starts with site. Design dialog then can commence with an inventive palette of materials, shapes, and expressions, allowing contemporary architectural expression to acclimatize to its place.

2000 years ago, the Romans terraced a hillside just north of Barcelona to grow grapes. Those formations still exist in the sleepy town of Teià and were the first place Berta Barrio and her husband and collaborator Josep Peraire took me to on our visit to her project, a small public library. The gesture of the terraced slopes and the green-roofed library are immediately apparent. The building yawns out of the landscape, gently funneling in passersby to a womb of knowledge. Inspired by a bookshelf, the eastward light shelves cut the morning glare while giving the entrance an engaging presence.

But the library's design intention is not to be secluded in a place to be lost in a book. The library turns and faces out to the town, to capture the weather, light, landscape, buildings, and movement of people. The crossing paths and the library's embedded setting encourage people to congregate. Visitors are summoned by the tall windows to feed on the view while taking a break from their reading. The library itself is about telling the story of the town, including the restoration of the oldest standing farmhouse just above. But that story is still not complete as the rooftop path, illuminated at night by the interior lights shining though the skylights, ends abruptly, and a rough dirt lot below waits for the vision to be realized.

ARCHITECT
SERGI GODIA & BERTA BARRIO ARQUITECTOS
TEIÀ, BARCELONA, SPAIN
COMPLETED 2009
1,167 SQUARE METERS

[BIBLIOTECA DE CAN LLAURADOR]

BERTA BARRIO

"For architecture in Spain, I think we have good universities, but we also have a good collection of modern architecture. In Spain, architects from modern times had to reveal the old architecture but with a new view, for instance, how the building has to work with the weather. A good example of this is the work of Josep Lluís Sert who also practiced in the US.

I wanted the library to feel natural, so even the green roof slopes from the middle. When you approach the library, the town is to your back. So maybe you forget the landscape, but when you enter the library you'll see that the space is organized to face the town. The most important thing in this area is the landscape of the town. It's something physical and it becomes an experience. These are the kind of things I look for when I first design. There was no path here before the library, so when I first visited the site the strongest element in the space was the view of the hills. If we put the library facing towards the ocean, you could be in Teià or you could be in another town; it is a nice view, but it's not about being here.

The reason for the structure in front is because the orientation is to the east, where you have sun in the morning. Since the sun in the morning is really low, we need this brise-soleil to keep the library cool. Here the problem is the heat in summer. This is the first time we used this kind of brise-soleil; it is very aggressive because of that eastern orientation. When we designed it we thought we would make something that reminds you of a bookshelf, with green books (laughs). But the design is not only to block the sun. I did not want people to sit in the back of the building; I wanted them to be in the front connected with the town visually. The problem is when you have a table that is only 70 millimeters high, then you have 4 meters of glass—I thought this would not feel very comfortable. So with this element in the facade, when you're

sitting down at the table you feel protected; it improves the scale of the space but does not block the view.

There is a large glass-enclosed meeting room to the back of the building that is directly connected to the outside. For this reason we put a patio in the back as well, which acts as an outdoor hall. When the space is full of university students, they can keep the room open until two in the morning. This is the solution we found to keep the library secure. Since this is the back of the building, we put in skylights that sit above the path across the roof. The lighting is on three circuits so it can adjust through the day.

We wanted to keep the raw concrete. It may not be perfect, but it's more important to see the material than for it to be perfect. The structure is also the finish for the library. Another important element is that we can see the cross and old farmhouse that is above. The cross designates the path down and through the library, which connects to the arcing corridor that runs along the library.

There is a designated children's area with books and space to play and to tell stories. And behind is an area for the staff and room for a small archive. Another thing that I like is because of the curve in the building you can only see the other parts of the building. The space is perhaps a little like a pavilion, and the interior can change in the future.

For us, the buildings are not only inside spaces; they are about the relationship between the inside and outside, about the people who are inside and the people who are outside. For instance, we designed a hospital with a park inside. Because it was not in a safe neighborhood, we decided to build it with an open facade with glass. People who walk along the street feel comfortable and more safe because they can be seen from inside by those who are in the waiting area. I think it's better for people

who are walking along the street but also for people waiting for the doctor because maybe they can be distracted a little bit. I prefer this kind of relationship with the buildings—I like to design a space about how I'll feel inside of it.

To organize this building in the park, we thought of the town's agriculture to establish the placement. The first element is the terraced vineyards on the hill. And the other element is the cultivation of flowers where you can see straight lines of color. We thought this was the best way to rebuild the slope we have here by making stairs and terraces like it was a vineyard.

Another important thing was how we decided to build the library below the old building, which was originally a farmhouse. This building dates from the 16th century, and we were afraid we couldn't build a great big building close to it because it is the essence of this place. So that also helped lead us to the principle of building, to a landscape language, rather than an architectural language. This form gives answers to concerns we had about putting a big building into the landscape. Because the green roof is pitched in, I think that trick makes you feel like this building belongs to this landscape. With this shape you get a less aggressive building.

We are not comfortable if we are just looking for shape when we design. We are confident that when we visit the place, work with the program, talk with the client, things come up in a natural way. This is very different from coming in with an agenda. It seems really simple and clear, but sometimes it's the most difficult to get to that resolution. The simplest things are the most difficult things. But I think it's a great way to work because in the end I feel proud of the work I've done. For me the best part is to come back to the building and talk to the people who work in or use the space. They are happy and it's great."

Adrià Goula

Adrià Goula

ARCHITECT
RAMÓN FERNANDEZ-ALONSO ARQUITECTO
ARCHIDONA, SPAIN
COMPLETED 2010
2,864 SQUARE METERS

[NEW CITY HALL ARCHIDONA]

Among the sea of olive groves in Southern Spain is the small, brilliantly white village of Archidona, one of many placed on the hillsides of the region. A high-speed rail line crosses the valley floor, and large wind turbines rest atop adjoining hills introducing our era to a place that has seen some of the earliest human settlers in Europe. Its town center is the octagonal Plaza Ochavada, surrounded with eateries and bars and often filled with lounging tourists and children playing, with the tiny old city hall making up a quarter of the plaza.

The city hall and cultural center expansion is a complex and contemporary incision into the space. The building's scope is difficult to grasp from the immediate exterior or from an adjacent hill where it illuminates like a beacon in the evening. It is best understood from the interior relationships with the original city hall. The dense building is navigated by four levels of program, which connect to the city's offices on top to the lower adjacent inclined street.

The transition inside between old and new is almost indistinguishable, but the addition is unapologetically contemporary. It tells the story of the city visually by introducing visitors to a sprawling view of the town and valley from the main gallery. Below is an auditorium sloped in unison with the street. Above are two floors of offices saturated with diffused light that comes through an orchestrated curtain of sandblasted glass.

RAMÓN FERNÁNDEZ-ALONSO

"In Spain we have good wine but it's not extraordinary—it is the reverse with architecture. In Portugal and in Spain you have very good architecture and very bad architecture as well. It is important in every project to find the right tools because it changes from context to context, and from program to program. The dialogue with the city, the people, the culture, the weather is necessary to achieve the final results.

The design tools they were talking about in Archidona specifically are the landscape and how the building stands in the landscape of the city. There is a lot of historical material and cultural material that needs to be used in the design. The landscape is reflected in the glass wall where it is seen from far away and within the context of the city. The cultural relationship is in the dimensions that we took from the existing buildings to create the new extension. The new building is a transition in both program and design from the existing building. The relation is best understood as you go through, so as the street goes down you also go down.

What I try to do is create an atmosphere much like making a movie. When you enter you have the compressed space, which is there also because you have to respect the existing building and work with four floors. I like to explain the building from the inside to the outside. This is because you can read the city from the inside. The first moments in the building are compressed as you can only see the buildings immediately next to you, but not the landscape far away. As you go through and up, then you will be able to take in the landscape and view from a higher level as the space opens up more. Because the exhibition area is a part of the city, it is good to juxtapose that view with

the space. So going through the space is like a movie pan because you are over all of the houses, which you view through the window. It is the way that things are composed in our thoughts. When you arrive at the ramp the landscape is static. The ramp is really a part of the street, so as you go up you are exposed to the exhibition and down you are hidden from it.

There are two important elements, the ramp and the glass curtain wall. They are both implemented to protect from the intensity of the sun. The ramp, which is on the middle level, pushes the building interior back from the sun, so acts as a brise-soleil. As you come closer to the glass you are more exposed to the sun, so the program is held back and elevated. Because the upper floors require more space, the double-skinned curtain wall has different kinds of angles in the glass. Those angles change according to the orientation of the sun, and the type of glass changes as well. They are like sunglasses for the building. This means that they do not need to use artificial light for most of the day, and the interior is quite comfortable.

Working with light is one of the basic features of architecture when you are designing. I have lived in the south of Spain since I was a child, so I'm used to the light, especially at sunset where it is the most difficult to work with. You can never design a brise-soleil that works for this, so it is quite difficult to dominate that light. It is also the most beautiful to introduce into a building because the color and the cast shadows are very different than during midday. It is something that you develop across your experience in your work, but it is also something related to the place where

you work or live. It is a part of the culture.

I learned from the Portuguese architect Álvaro Siza that a complicated topography is not the problem that it may seem at first. You turn it into an opportunity. So for the building in Archidona, you have different levels so you can exit at different elevations. It may not be a question that you need to design with the topography, but it can be a valuable design tool. So the topography can create opportunities that you would not have had before. It has been said about Siza's architecture that his buildings are like cats: they climb up and down to find the best place to take in the sun. So the context gives you the tools you need.

When I think about architecture I think about the place. The most important thing is that the building belongs to the place, that the architecture is responsive to the context. Architecture must be sustainable by nature. If you are designing a building, it must belong to a place, and so then it will be also able to handle anything across time. Sustainable architecture should be understood this way. It is not so much about designing something that is modern or efficient necessarily. So, architecture must be sustainable in a place but also in time. We think of architectural time as related to technological developments. If there is a need for technology it should use that technology in context. There are many options, and some of them are very useful, but it is important to be selective of the technologies you use in your design.

There is a need to explain what you intend to do before doing it, always. If not, everyone will attack you. I always explained to people in the university how the project would work, what its impact will be in the city. The beauty of the architecture is a result of its coherence. You will always find something attractive if it has some order, that it's something that you can understand. Architecture is a service, which means that you are not working for yourself but working for others. One of the most important things to design and think about is how people will feel in your building, how they interact, and if they are going to enjoy it or not. When they come out of the building they can look at it, and in the context of the city they'll understand why it is like that. When that is successful, you feel rewarded.

There is a shared point of view, but it was understood that they are the ones who are using the space, so you must think about their needs while designing. When you're designing someone's house, they always want more and more. So here we have a small auditorium, a small exhibition room, some offices; so we gave them everything they wanted. But the town hall is not very big; it had to be designed for the dimensions of the city. The auditorium only has 300 seats, but that is large enough for this town. The exhibition room provides the panorama of the landscape.

The building should be used in different ways like your own house. It is designed to have a kitchen, living room, bedroom, and so on. It does not mean that the living room cannot be transformed into something else at that moment. Architecture should work like that, and here in Spain I try to design buildings so that they can be used in very different ways, not only the first one that was proposed.

The intention was not to create an icon for the city, but it does work that way. There are some friends who said they did not know about the project but when they came towards the city and saw it in the distance they tried to find out what it was. So the project is contemporary in that it is unexpected, and architecture must be contemporary. 🎔

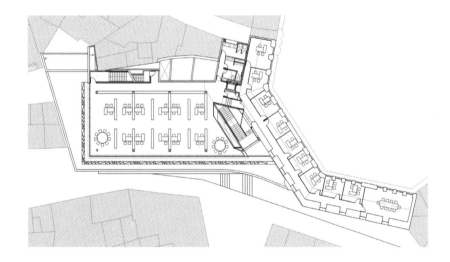

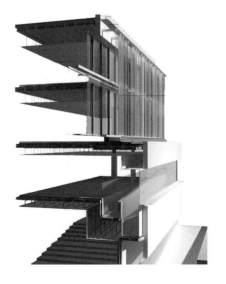

ARCHITECT
MCDONOUGH + PARTNERS
BARCELONA, SPAIN
IN DEVELOPMENT
19,500 SQUARE METERS

[FERRER RESEARCH & DEVELOPMENT CENTER]

WILLIAM MCDONOUGH

" Our first design for the lab was two towers basically connected by an atrium and they "wiggled" up. The column floors actually rotated as the floors were being poured, so it had this movement as it rose. It was the same form used over and over again, but it had this organic element. For us that was very much a part of being in Barcelona with the tradition of Gaudí, tile, and things like that. So it was a clay building really, almost like pottery, a pulled form from clay shaped by hand. It was almost like two dancers. As you came into Barcelona from the airport it would be prominent. It would be in a very orthogonal set of blocks, to the right of the hospital. So we thought of this organic form of tile and clay with a view moving through the middle of it. I thought of it as very Barcelona, very grounded because it had an organic choreography.

As we were working on it there was this one moment I'll never forget. This is a funny set of leaps, the synaptic space that's not necessarily coherent, it's more improvisation. It's more jazz than, say, a structured beat. We are back in the office and one of the designers working on the floor plan said, "You know, Bill, I'm having trouble with the budget on the flooring because we are laying out all of the tiles." This was because of the radial nature of the floor plan. It's a problem we solved for the design of the building shape economically because we're actually using the same forms for each floor and just kicking them for each level. It's very practical construction actually, but a beautiful shape. So they are looking at the floors and they said we have to cut all the tiles in a radial pattern to meet the floor plan and meet the walls, which are coming together in sort of a pie shape, which makes it very expensive. I said, "Why are we doing that, let's just place the tiles down first."

I like to design the buildings so they can become anything in the future. Even though it's labs, this building could become housing some other day when you don't need a lab. That's why Rome was not built in a day, but the buildings that were built in Rome can last for centuries. Not only are they robustly made, but also easy to repair and adaptable to many human purposes. Like Soho in New York, these buildings were meant for manufacturing and warehousing, but they have tall windows for deep daylighting because they had gas lamps. They had high ceilings because of the bad air of these lamps and for hot air in the summer to be at the ceiling. Then there's good ventilation where you can open the top and bottom of the windows for good air movement because you have that height. The buildings have thermal mass so they can be cooled in the evenings, and they have good acoustics. So those buildings can become anything – housing, art studios, offices, loft apartments, whatever. Over time that's how community can be maintained and reformed as buildings adapt to various human purposes.

So I was looking at this building and thinking I don't want to lay this out as laboratories forever. So why don't I just make a tile floor that is general and then we put in the walls afterward so you have this beautiful underlying pattern in simplicity of floor. And I thought what if we had a beautiful pattern, something that was designed with a larger field? Why would you want just a pattern for a hallway or rooms? Why not have something beautiful? So, I

decided it should be a butterfly wing and we can lay tile by number. So we started to pixelate the ancient butterflies of Barcelona, especially the ones that are going extinct. It's a very urgent question for me. Why don't we have a building that celebrates local biodiversity rather than just talking about reducing carbon or something? And this is what I mean by quirky because the butterfly is still there but you just see it in a different iteration (laughs). Once I had it I couldn't let go of it, it's so charming as a notion.

It all comes out from this crazy improvisation when you're free to listen to songs. If that was our floor plan, what if we take the atrium and use it as a hatchery for the ancient butterflies? Why not go to work every day and see butterflies hatch. Wouldn't that be more interesting than importing rainforest plants when I can watch beautiful things restore the biodiversity of the city? Now we started thinking about the building as a butterfly hatchery. You get into a lot of issues with that because you don't want them to get sucked into a return air duct, and you are a laboratory so you have hygiene issues, and it goes on. So it is fun to speculate how you would live with butterflies. These are just the curiosities that drive innovation. But the butterflies just capture me.

In the middle of all that, the Spanish economy collapses. The government tells the pharmaceuticals that they have to cut the prices of everything they do by some monstrous proportion, and I think a couple of big companies went out of business after this. A very dramatic emergency of economic distress. Our client Sergi Ferrer-Salat, who is a real renaissance man, and this is the key to this whole thing, is a jazz

aficionado and understands improvisation. When you improvise there are two things I discovered in our work you have to remember. The thing that kills improv is the word "no." If you're passing a tune back and forth, or in theater a rapporté, if you try something out and somebody says no then it's over. The other thing that can stop an improv is a revelation. In the middle of it someone says, "Oh, my God," and it stops because they're having a private moment. All of a sudden you can't breathe because we had to stop because he couldn't afford to build that with the market.

Having such a lovely time speculating about what it means for a building to restore butterflies, I had a revelation. Of course I can design a building that restores biodiversity. Like when I did the Ford Rouge vegetated roofed building in Dearborn, Michigan, I had to talk to the board to get approval; so, I started by saying, "This building is for the birds." And that is true. Then we showed them the economics and we were done because I saved them $35 million capital, and 4% margin is the equivalent of $900 million in cars. That's local, they are a car company and these are fiduciaries. So there you are, but it was for the birds that migrated over that plant. Everywhere I go I will leave behind a wetland, or oxygen producing things, not asphalt, which are really two words assigning blame. So this is what the upcycle is about, the celebration of abundance. There are so many people involved in doing things that are less bad, like reducing car emissions. It's all very nice, but you're saying what you're not. You're saying what you don't want to be, not what you want to be.

So what happened when the various

economic resources were reassessed and the needs for research and development for the company were re-articulated, we all got together and decided that the building should be two-thirds of the size given the realities of the marketplace. The budget had to be extremely contained in terms of luxuries—the curve had to be simplified. The approach we took, which I think is germane to your thesis, was that while staring at it at first we were going to hold onto the butterflies, it's too cool. As Louis Pasteur said, "Chance favors the prepared mind." We're going to be very practical with it. So at that moment I realized what the nicest way to do it was because I've been looking at butterfly hatcheries for about a year. Every time I saw something or heard about it I went to look at it. I found one in Costa Rica that was really quite lovely. It was a small little place in the jungle, and

basically there was a glass wall in the room where the visitors would be. And then there were shelves every two feet with chrysalis that would be attached. Then there was a glass door on the exterior where keepers would come and release the butterflies. They have these net bags which they carefully encouraged the butterflies to fly into, and then they would release them.

So, I thought, this is it. The lobby can have two glass walls; there's an inside glass wall and an outside glass wall. The outside glass walls are a set of giant doors that can be opened by the children. So, during the week when people come in to work, they will walk by butterflies hatching in the lobby. They're not in my return ducts or anything. The children can come in on the weekends and open the doors on the outside and release the butterflies into the fauna.

One of the grand scenarios is that the children will be able to ask the parks department, "What happened to the habitat for the butterflies?" Some of these species are very rare now to the point where they are counted down to the individually tracked. That is how sad this is. So, a year and half after I propose this, there is an article in the newspaper in Barcelona saying we are losing all our butterflies. That bolstered what we were proposing. The children can now say to the parks department this is what the butterflies need. And then go to the highway department because the highway goes out to the airport and say all the growth around the bridges, those weeds are habitat.

If it is a tower, then we can have this beautiful gesture. If it's not a tower and it is a much chunkier looking thing because of the proportioning, why do I have to have a

building that looks the same on all sides? Our original building is curved, and the south side is where solar and shading were. On the north side it had green walls because they would not dry out. We can take the graywater from the building and grow various plants on the side. That building had that, and I wanted to build on it. We made the east side, which gets sun in the morning, our biological nutrient wall. So that wall is all wood; you inhabit it with balconies and trees and shade. It's a part of the biological nutrient world as far as materials. Then on the southwest, which is quite severe with high sun, are solar collectors, where we make our energy. Then the northwest, which is very hot in the afternoon in the summer, is the butterfly wall. It has vertical shading in the colors and patterns of one of my favorite butterflies, little butterfly wings all over the wall that are colorful and do the

shading to keep the direct sun out of the laboratories. The north side is all greenery, watered by the graywater of the building. It is tuned to the graywater of the building because we know how much water there is.

All of a sudden you have a building with completely different facades because there are four completely different orientations. To the southeast we face residential, to the south we face the highway. That's where the technical nutrient solar collectors are. To the northwest we face the highway and the buildings in the distance, that's why they get to look at a beautiful thing that sparkles like a butterfly wing. And in the city they get to look back to the elevation of this green facade because it's on the north side, and they can say, "Oh, there's a building that's producing oxygen and purifying water." And that's the butterfly building.

It's funny how the building kept morphing. It's like it was a caterpillar, curvaceous and solid, and then it turned into this diaphanous, colorful, light thing. So the building design actually went through the same metamorphosis a butterfly does, which is kind of sweet.

There's the old line in modernism that form follows function. We like to think that the next level of that is form follows evolution. The next one beyond that is form follows celebration. So for me the Gaudí-like proposal was form following evolution with the Barcelona aesthetic and the deployment of various materials in the tower and so on. Then once we had butterflies it became a celebration. For me it's about the evocation of human intention. I think that's why the idea that form follows celebration is so important. 🙶

ARCHITECT
CANVAS ARQUITECTO
SALAMANCA, SPAIN
2007
5,750 SQUARE METERS

[INSTITUTE OF NEUROSCIENCES OF CASTILLA Y LEÓN]

Salamanca is home to the world's third oldest university, which was established in 1134 and has recently begun expanding its research with dedicated satellite labs. The Institute of Neurosciences is near the fringe of the compact city, resting among typically blocky residential low-rise buildings.

As a reaction to the bland construction of the neighborhood, the project cuts into the sloping site and replaces the original landscape with a new one. The entry is nestled in the back of the site providing ingress through the cut landscape. The vegetated roof is punctuated with four skylights and two light wells, and skirted in a generous deck. On top, a formal rectangular massing, shrouded in a translucent skin, overlooks the greenery. The city is surprisingly chilly in wintertime, so the upper volume acts as a solar thermal collector feeding the main floor with solar heat.

Its programming formulation is influenced by the architecture of the brain. The distribution of the spaces is in sections. A lecture hall and learning environments are in the upper formal building, a place of rest and connection to the exterior sits below. On the main level is a distributed open network of workspaces fed by a circular open hall. The subterranean level houses the testing labs. The entire building, with the exception of the labs, is day lit with automated lighting turned on only well after the beginning of dusk.

JUAN VICENTE

I investigate with this architecture because the Institute is about investigation. The architecture is investigation because it wasn't all there when I designed it. We worked very closely with the university in developing this project. The design came very quickly, in four or five months, so it was very fast. That is the best way to approach a project, otherwise there can be too much information. This way the design is very natural for me. The plans may look complex but in my head it is very simple, because if it is not simple in my head, the project is not possible.

The investigation of light through the space is very interesting. The light, the height, the section, is all very cinematic because in the moment, you see a distinct perspective of the space with the architecture of the building. This kind of complexity is interesting for us. If anything is okay or if it is not okay, I do not know until we build it (laughs). For instance, at this moment the way the light comes through the ramp to the spaces below is the intention of the design of the architecture. But for me, the way the light works is not okay because it does not illuminate the lower spaces as I

would prefer. Now this investigation will be left for other projects.

The program is complex; the entrance, the ramp, the movement through the space, the moments a person experiences in the building are very important for us. It is not a static building. It is like a neuron and neurological pattern. In the first designs of the elevation, I wanted to bring this pattern. I wanted the program to be influenced by the structure of the brain.

The space is planned around the work of the Institute. The research of the brain is very interesting to me and that has influenced the design. Working with the director was very informative to see the idea of the architecture of the brain, the neurological study in the formation of the cranium.

The contour of the building is very irregular with the islands and the lightscape, so the interior spaces are very formal boxes. Below in the earth are the labs, which are closed off from the landscape. Upstairs are the deck, lecture hall, class rooms, and the green roof, so the formal spaces are very distant from the work in the labs directly below. This was the investigation for me of this project.

In the section it is very important how the green roof integrates into the site. The formation of the building mimics the original slope. I wanted it to be distinct visually from the buildings around it and the city beyond. And the box on top is visually very formal as well, very rectangular. This houses the offices and lecture room, which are very formal spaces.

For me, the most important part of the project was the relationship between these levels. These are two worlds that are very different: the interior work of the ground floor, the labs, and the work up in the air in the landscape, and the light for the conference space, the café, and the deck. One is very focused and the other is an open investigation.

We need the project to draw attention back to the ground because the city around us is very conventional. We are creating an artificial landscape, the topography is remodeled, and that replaces what was here before. Before this, it belonged to the green inclined plain. 🙿

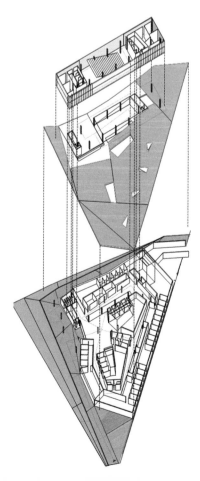

[SPAIN WRAPS] Institute of Neurosciences of Castilla Y Leon

As a police station, the design is as subversive as it is visually compelling and environmentally appropriate. The architects employed the panopticon architectural device developed in the late 18th century for guards to scan an entire prison cell ward from a single point. The intent is not for criminals in this case, the holding cells are below ground, but for citizens to observe the police. There are few opaque vertical surfaces, except in the case of interview rooms and private offices. By pushing the meeting areas outside of the scrim-wrapped volume the intent is further stretched. The occupants are literally over the city they serve, a not so subtle gesture to remind them of the citizenry. In this way, the police station is not a fortification but a beacon.

The building is pushed back from the street, and a substantial open courtyard is provided for outdoor gathering, although under the surveillance of many cameras. To further temper the volume, organic materials in the form of gabion cages full of river stones provide a gentle transition from the building to the ground. That design temperament is brought inside with ample wood, flashes of color, and generous skylights.

The building's arrangement expresses great modernist discipline with a strict grid as a guideline. The second skin reflects the ambient light during the day, protecting the extensive glazed curtain wall from the solar gain. In the evening, the building's personality inverts and becomes wholly transparent, providing a welcome refuge to those in need of police services.

ARCHITECT
VOLUAR ARQUITECTURA
FUENCARRAL-EL PARDO, MADRID, SPAIN
2008
6,770 SQUARE METERS

[COMISARÍA FUENCARRAL-EL PARDO]

BORJA LOMAS

"The police station is designed to be friendlier to the citizens. They like it because this space is like a gift to the city because it is designed to be approachable by the local inhabitants. I think it is important to create a space between the people and the police. When Mies van der Rohe designed the Seagram building, he provided a square in front. To put a square between the streets and the building creates a new space, which is good for the image of the building, it is more iconic. At the lower level of the building is a stereotomic part, which is like the ground, and above the architecture is tectonic. The problem with a police station is to separate the public space with the private space because of security. The design is classic in that the first floor is used to separate these spaces. The building is also a response to the topography of the street's slope downward, so there are two different levels. We wanted the building to adapt to the situation as we always worry about the site. There are other architects who do not necessarily care about the environment they place the building in.

The forms of the building are very abstract because here the city is not very attractive. I didn't have many references of buildings in the area. It is a play of taking a space from the inside and putting it to the outside. The spaces cantilevered outside are meeting rooms for the police. I wanted to make it so that when the police were together, they are not in the building but are looking to the city to be more sensitive to the citizens. So, maybe sometimes you forget you are police and instead you are a citizen in this space. So maybe you have to get out of your regular day and think about the neighborhood around you.

The skin of the building reflects the daylight, so at sunset the building changes, and in the morning it changes. The building is always changing, and if you move, the intensity of the light changes. It is also nice to see how the skin disappears in the evening. I very much like this effect. During the day the skin filters the light in, and nights it casts light. It is upside down between day and night. We wanted it to act like a lighthouse, so it is a point of reference for the people who need to go to the police station at night. If something bad happened, you want to be able to find it easily.

I think using natural light is a good way to save energy. The skin responds to this environment because in the summer it can be very hot and acts as a filter. All the boxes are the same in the building except to the west because there the light is very strong. For the scrim, each one is sized to accommodate a specific amount of light into a particular space. When we designed the police station we wanted to structure it with the light. So the structure is designed to communicate the light. In a way, it is a game where sometimes you can see it, but sometimes you can't. If you have too much daylight it is not good, and if you do not have enough light it is also not good, so it is a mix of these concepts. To be at the limit of these concepts is the richest place for architecture. I like to play with things that change because architecture is often something considered to be solid.

In summer the scrim is a filter but allows some light. In the winter it can provide a warm layer of air against the building. The screens are perforated in a way that allows them to provide more shade in the summer, and in winter more light can come through.

So the outer skin provides protection all year. We select different filters for whether we need more or less light inside. For an office we may block more light but for a bathroom will let in more light. We do not want to be too restrictive so that the program can change—we don't want to limit the way the building can be used.

I am very skeptical of architects who call themselves green and use a lot of equipment. They call them intelligent buildings, where computers control everything. You can spend a lot of money on these technologies to solve problems that you solve with simple systems that are passive. For instance, I'd like to see buildings in other countries like those in Turkey that use chimneys to capture the wind, and that becomes the architecture of the city. They are solving problems without energy, or more precisely using the environmental energy. I believe we can use the knowledge of the tradition but cast it in a modern way with a modern design. We are practicing in the 21st century, so the language of your architecture must be modern. But, we must use the knowledge we have learned over time to create better architecture. The screen is actually very traditional architecture that can be seen mainly in the south of Spain. It would be made out of wood, and I think it was originally from the Arabic architectural tradition. From the inside you can see out clearly but you cannot see in.

For the interior we wanted a panoptic effect so that no matter where you are, you can see through the building. The effect is most pronounced at the top levels. There are a lot of places in the building where you can change the program to accommodate for the changing needs of the owner. The building must be flexible in order to adapt as an answer to the questions of their needs. All the partitions of the interior are modular, and the floor plans are kept relatively simple.

I've studied the work of firms who are changing the concept of the office. There are studies of how natural light increases the productivity of the occupants. Also, having a view through a window makes the worker feel as though the company takes care of them. They're not a machine but a person. So, I think there are a number of things that can increase the productivity of people while they are working. We put in automatic screens in the conference room but I don't know why they don't use them. They instead installed cheap blinds.

I like to reference things that I study. Mondrian was an influence for the ventilation design in the parking garage. This is an important thing for an architect: don't just study architecture, but study everything because there is always a relationship between things, and you do not know where the ideas can come from. And because this is life, it may not just be art but it could be geology, sociology, or poetry; so, I think is very important to have feedback and carry all this knowledge with you. The hardest thing is to show architecture in a simple way. It feels like the building is floating, that it is going against gravity. I like that because it is not just about the human reality now, it's a way to look forward to the future. 🙰

Angel Baltanás

Angel Baltanás

Ángel Baltanás

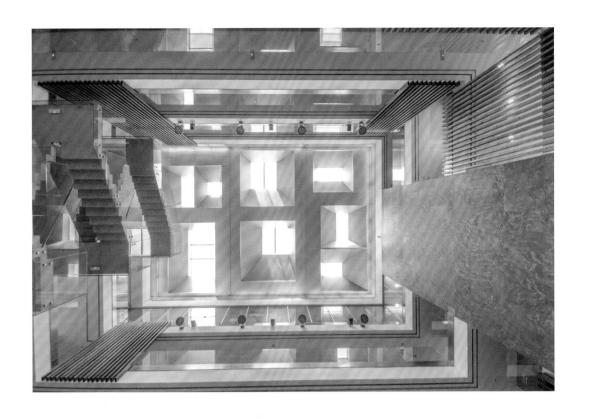

E8 is a midsized commercial office building in a growing technology office park of two dozen facilities in a green field site on the outskirts of Vitoria-Gasteiz. Its transformation from being an office building to an abstracted imprint of the land and sky is superlative. Large facets of glass draw the reflection of the sky down to the earth, as though the building is in the process of disappearing. The intention of the facade, formally, is to create an impression of the land before development. The altruistic gesture is almost a way to make amends to all of the awkwardly conceived architecture plopped on the fresh development.

But good design is also as much about the way a building works. The second skin admirably performs as a parasol providing solar control and wind protection, which, in turn, significantly reduces operating energy. It also provides easy access via scaffolding to the exterior for maintenance. While the program is strictly an open-floor office space, the envelope is ringed with operable windows buffeted from gusts by the outer skin, which is a rare gesture for this type of program. Small but grateful reminders of nature are embedded in the landscape such as a nascent forest in the parking lot and a garden wrapping the building perimeter. A small oak-forested hill and open plains adjoin two sides of the site.

ARCHITECT
COLL-BARREU ARQUITECTOS
VITORIA-GASTEIZ SPAIN
2011
13,000 SQUARE METERS

[E8 BUILDING]

JUAN COLL-BARREU | DANIEL GUTIÉRREZ ZARZA

JCB: We thought that the building itself could work as kind of a recording machine for the landscape. The area will transform with the construction of new buildings, but E8 is in a nice corner of the business park. We thought that the forms of the building serve the purpose to not only reflect the sky and the landscape of the forest, but also contain the memory of the natural environment before the new buildings, to remember the natural surroundings of the area. I think that works because of the reflection of the sky and because of the garden inside the building between the north and south entrance on the ground floor. It's a way to recall what was there before. It is a vision of its natural environment and a sense of landscape. But it's a transitional landscape between nature and the city. It's also a transition in terms of time because it sits between the previously all-natural landscape and the future construction of the area. So, it is a transition of both space and time.

The entrance is a kind of relaxing area between the building and the walk from your car. In the middle of the building we can see the structural vertical columns, and as you walk through some columns run at 45 degrees. This is how I indicate that you are in the bridge of the building; this way there is always a dynamic between you and the structure. The structure will help you know where you are in the building. You know how the forces are modeled in the building, and it will help you understand the outdoor shape of the building. At that kind of level, the building communicates with you in terms of the structure; it is an interface between you and its elements.

We like to use colors that are not colors, blacks and whites. This allows people to bring in their own things because these are offices for rent. We do like to make the building different from a normal office though, so here you have this ceramic built-in bench for a rest area or stainless steel doors in the bathrooms. When your hand is touching the building, it tacitly changes as you are in contact. I think this is nice too. When the owners show the building, they always take the prospective client to the bathroom because of the quality of the space. I think that we forget we have natural relationships in our life, for example, water. Water is not just a tool to wash your hands; it's important to connect it to the natural systems. It is the same for light, we must celebrate that. So it's important to not just consider the landscape but to embed natural elements into the building.

You can see the trees dividing the parking lot. We are waiting for the growth of the trees, and when they mature it will be a nice place, a place where the environment is integrated into the lot. We did not want a huge parking lot like a commercial center where you park every day; this one is pretty big. When the trees mature they will form rooms—it is a very simple system. So now you can park inside of a sort of room with green walls.

Outside is a catwalk for maintenance. The building can easily be cleaned by walking around it. There are many windows you can open, but they are narrow in order to provide security. Of course every desk can have its own window to open. The client did not want this—they do not like people walking on the outside to be able to control the windows.

DGZ: Because the offices are for different enterprises, and there are spaces for rent, security was very important.

JCB: You can imagine we had problems with the mechanical engineers; they would prefer a perfect bubble. We had conversations, so they worked with us. We do not only need perfect climate conditions and lighting, but we also need contact with the outdoors. So opening a window is a way to increase our level of comfort.

DGZ: It creates a relationship between the office and the outside. With the trees changing color, it is very nice to work here. The important thing to note is the width of the office and its connection to the outside. We are paying more attention to nature than we usually would for an office building. For us, this building is in a very different context than other buildings in the center of the city. We need to express that.

JCB: When people see this, in, say, an architectural magazine, they are only concerned with iconic insertions. It is really about a sense of relationship between people in the building and the building in nature. We think that is the important thing. Reality has many levels, but in our daily life we usually forget about those levels. We are worried about important things, of course, but there are many things we forget about. So our buildings are designed to remember those things.

ARCHITECT
COLL-BARREU ARQUITECTOS
BILBAO, SPAIN
2008
9,200 SQUARE METERS

[BASQUE HEALTH DEPARTMENT HEADQUARTERS]

Bilbao is known for both its working-class ethos and the home of the Guggenheim Museum, which jump started a movement of contemporary iconic public architecture. The new Basque Health Department Headquarters knits these two qualities together with a highly functional and striking expression of contemporary place making in the core of the city. The program condenses many satellite offices of the health department into a single space to improve efficiency as well as collate services for the public. They wanted a building that stood out in the city, to demarcate the services the department provided to the citizens. The architects responded with a finely-tuned floor plan wrapped in an extraordinary fractured facade.

The double skin is suspended on a stainless steel scaffold protecting the glass curtain envelope and walkout balconies, which are common in the city. Building codes enacted 150 years prior dictated the shape of the building, which is echoed throughout the dense urban corridor, with mediocre results in the post-war era. The true gift is in how the building functions. The second skin wards off noise, glaring heat, and cool ocean fog while catalyzing a connection with the interior to the exterior.

The contemplative character of the headquarters is what inserts it back into the city. It is an homage to place. The fragmented glass reflects the neighbors and reinterprets the cityscape while drawing the sky to street level. When I was photographing the building two other photographers appeared and were simulalry engrossed with their ocular discovery.

JUAN COLL-BARREU

"Basque country is a good place to have more transparent buildings—it is a good thing for people to receive the sun. We could take advantage of that with the Health Department Headquarters because it is on a corner lot. It is in the center of the city and a prime area for offices. It is on orthogonal streets, a typical grid, in a 19th-century town. We felt that the directions of the city are not only through the streets. You see, the activity of the city is very dynamic. There're not only two directions; you can look up, you can see people across the way, cars moving, people crossing the street, people who look from windows to the street. So there are a lot of directions. The fragmented facade is a way to explain the multi-directional nature of the city and lift that dynamic action. It brings the in sky as well, and I think that is important. Due to the multiple geometries, you are folded into the city visually, and the city makes its way into the building. So, communication happens between the city and the building, and, of course, people on the street and people working in the building.

The traditional vernacular uses balconies, operable windows, and ornate facades in order to have a connection to the city. But in the last 20 years, buildings have flat facades so they do not have as strong a relationship as the vernacular buildings. That's why I believe that the facets actualize that relationship, make it more real and more present and reclaim that lost relationship between buildings and the city. Because of restrictive codes, we placed a tower on the building, but we do not want to go back to the vernacular. The thing is to find positive things in our buildings, but we do not design for nostalgia. For instance, each floor has a balcony that you can step onto. It is an idea of making a kind of exchange space on each floor between

the indoors in the outdoors. The space is different on each floor since each floor is different, so the exchange that happens is different. That space will be fine for working or rest or break during the workday; it is a place for plants and flowers. And, it's a place for the city to enter the work environment. I think this is a positive idea because the work environment is not an isolated bubble; instead, it's a place that belongs to the city. We work with the client in that sense, so that occupants are well connected to the building, and with open spaces, it creates a very friendly environment for interaction. For example, in most office buildings it's not easy to realize if it is raining outside or if it's sunny. We thought that it could be possible to keep that connection.

The old-fashioned city code was created in 1862 when buildings were made out of wood and brick. This was for structural reasons, but it is very difficult for reinforced concrete to take the same form. We must repeat the lines of the neighboring buildings, and we must have a tower in the quarter like the adjacent buildings. And finally, the building must step back from the frontage for the last two floors. That is a very complicated requirement and makes a very uncomfortable building for office use. So, we looked for a construction system that was very conducive to these floor plates and remains open and transparent for the workspace and the city. This second skin also helped us meet the city code. But it does express and enliven the dynamic reality of the town.

The facade works in other ways as well: it is a sort of isolation tool for the sun, but also for the noise. It is a paradox; the building is more protected from outside elements while also being more connected than a typical office building. When we were

deciding on this facade we felt that it must work not only architecturally but in terms of energy. In wintertime it is extra protection for the building, it creates a buffer, which maintains a layer of heat on the glass envelope. In the summertime it has the opposite effect because the separation helps maintain a cooler condition on the inner facade. So now we can save on air conditioning.

That means we can design a climate system without a conventional air-conditioning system. Instead, we can use piped water along the ceilings for hot or cold, and we can put conditioning in difficult places in the building or take the heat from one part and distribute it to another part. This is the first time we used this mechanical system after we saw some projects in Germany. This is also very good news for the health of the people who are working in the building because we do not recirculate air but introduce fresh air when we need it. It is also quieter and has a gentler air circulation, so it is more comfortable. By saving energy, we are able to have substantial savings in the cost of conditioning the building. So, we have two improvements, one for health and the other for energy savings.

There is a third element that is also very important: we can save construction costs because we can build a smaller building. Because we do not need room for a conventional air-conditioning system, we can save 80 centimeters per floor, more or less, since we do not need big ducts. This means that we can build one more floor in the building. In this case, the health department does not need another office in another part of the city. So the economic benefit is very important in saving the cost of the construction and the carbon footprint of another office."

Aleix Bague

Aleix Bague

[MEXICO

EMBEDS]

The practice of adapting our built environment underground is perhaps one of the oldest of human concepts of shelter. Our ancestors spent many generations in the embrace of caves for protection, and then later, actively dug shelter out of the raw earth. The Ancient Pueblo dwellings of the Southwest United States, Cappadocia in Turkey, and Buddhist Mogao Caves along the Silk Road in China may be more famous examples. Nearly every region on earth has been touched by humans using the ground as shelter. Now the idea of using the earth as a place to locate urban habitation is mainly set aside for transportation or services. For a modern development nearly all of the design concerns are about what takes place above the surface, neglecting the potential of using what is below.

In warmer climates the argument for embedded architecture is simple. It is much cooler underground than above, and vernacular architecture reflects this insight. Think of the housing in Tunisia, where the filming of Luke Skywalker's desert planet home took place. The homes called troglodyte were built into the ground around hand dug or natural pits. The rhythms of life occurred above or below depending on the season. Now the constraints of buildings, especially in urban environments, are about maximizing space and program, and reducing energy. Architects are rediscovering the practical and aesthetic benefits of embedding a building into the earth as it provides more opportunities for use of the space on top while reducing the imprint on the landscape. From an energy perspective, heating, and especially cooling loads are steeply reduced. Pro-

viding a space that is not 'cave like', but instead airy and light filled, is a significant challenge.

Mexico is becoming a proving ground for such architecture, and my first hint of this was the Earthscaper which earned BNKR Arquitectura an honorable mention in the 2010 eVolo Skyscraper Competition. It is an audacious proposal to turn the famous Zocalo Plaza in Mexico City into a 65 story inverted pyramid plunging into the ground, with a glass roof at ground level to serve as the plaza. The idea was salient enough to go viral in the media, which is rare for radical architecture proposals. While the Earthscraper is a speculation, Papalote Verde Monterrey is a newly completed subterranean children's Museum by Iñaki Echeverria. Sprawling beneath the landscape, the museum's glass crevasse keeps occupants connected to the outside. Back in Mexico City, adjacent to the instant landmark, Museo Soumaya by Fernando Romero, is a similarly scaled theater by Ensemble Architects. It is inserted completely beneath a street level atrium. The theater's subtractive design is as compelling as its terrestrial shiny neighbor, and avoids a competition of attention.

Just as important, these projects are climate adapted for the hot Mexican summer days. For a commercial building , the significant heat load of an outer skin absorbing radiation during the day is largely removed. Since the earth's thermal mass regulates the building's internal temperature, engineers can reduce the size of air conditioning at peak occupancy. This shift of the cooling burden to throughout the day lowers the overall carbon impact and better matches the building's energy consumption with renewable energy output.

There are only a few noteworthy embedded projects in the burgeoning region, but the conversation with KMD's Roberto Velasco makes clear there is a tremendous appetite. KMD's sunken Garden Santa Fe has sparked over a half a dozen fresh proposals using similar tactics. Placed on the southwest edge of the 10th largest urban area in the world, the satellite city of Santa Fe exemplifies of the unregulated sprawl of the last decades, where private money vastly outpaced public infrastructure. In response to these conditions, Garden Santa Fe is a peculiar hybrid of basic infrastructure needs, a re-envisioning of contemporary retail, topped with a re-born green space. Each element is not necessarily noteworthy individually, but the process of stacking and embedding these programs in the ground, while maintaining the nature of a precious open space, is a compelling lesson in urban adaptation for Mexico City. Urban land use pressure adds more and more needs to the same place, so realizing layers of use facilitates design options. The building code in Mexico, which does not count underground program against a project's size limit, provides that opportunity.

Embedded architecture is not about hiding buildings, but about better intigrating them to the human scale. Since you still need to provide light and egress it means the architecture is an insertion, rather than an act of camouflage. A house underground in a pristine landscape is a much different aesthetic realization than, say, a subterranean retail development in an urbanized locus. One is about creating less disruption to the landscape, the other is about providing more use in dense surroundings. The need for public green spaces and infrastructure merge elegantly with underground architecture. Embedded architecture can be a kind of radical form of enhanced land use. By inserting program below, the surface is allowed to facilitate public good. A park or plaza is always preferable to a big box. In allows vegetation to be inserted where the humans are. Placing trees on top of buildings is a popular architectural gesture now, but to walk up and smell a flowering Primavera Tree is much more engaging. The viewscape is maintained, allowing a city to breath, you can see the sky or where you are going.

By embedding architecture the way people can transverse a city is enhanced by merging commercial spaces with transportation and open space. The role of design becomes more subtle, engineering more complex. It is subtle in that clever solutions for egress and day lighting force architects to be inventive. The complication of engineering, services, and excavation creates a higher cost than typical buildings. When I presented the concept of the Earthscraper to a group of large scale developers in Amsterdam someone asked, "How much does it cost?" The answer is a lot, but risking answering a question with a question my response was, "How much value does it create?"

The story of Garden Santa Fe starts with a parking lot. While not usually how a sustainable project initiates, the immense underground parking structure bottoms out at 33 meters beneath the street, placing the ubiquitous automobile where it belongs, well below human and natural habitation. Set above is a typical mall, only its three stories are also subterranean.

The architectural device of inserting three full story glass atriums essentially brings the outdoors to the underground floor plates. The circular courtyards, complete with live trees at the bottom and second level of the mall, provides a release from what would otherwise be a claustrophobic environment. Then there is the copious amount of daylight they usher inside.

The energy density of the mall is 60% of typical retail spaces in part from the natural lighting, low energy equipment, and the reduced need for air conditioning, with some supplemental solar electricity. An extensive rain collection system and on site grey water treatment and water reuse process makes a similar impact in water consumption.

Lastly, there is the park. It is modest in scope for an urban center but as the surrounding area has been swallowed whole by development, the vegetated refuge will become a core social asset.

ARCHITECT
KMD ARCHITECTS | ARQUITECTOMA
MEXICO CITY, MEXICO
2014
76,108 SQUARE METERS

[GARDEN SANTA FE]

ROBERTO VELASCO

"The project is quite audacious, and a new concept to the region actually, because it's the first time there is a commercial underground retail venue. The story is about how we and the developer Arquitectoma untied the knot to make this a reality. Our office is just opposite of the park so I know the area well. Back in 1985 this was where all the debris from the earthquake was placed. Santa Fe was typically a mining area, so it was nothing but sand mines. But after the earthquake the local government decided to use this place to deposit destroyed buildings from the downtown area. By that time they realized the place had a huge potential to be developed, so in 1987 they invited Universidad Iberoamericana to come over and become a flagship project for the area, so they built a huge University just opposite of Garden Santa Fe.

The government was very clear on developing this site themselves so they hired a very prominent politician who started a public-private agency to put this all together. Back then nobody knew that this would be so successful over time because it was very cheap land at the time. Now it is a huge business center, very much a typical business district with around 400,000 people. When KMD came to Mexico in 1993 we decided to set up our offices in one of the few buildings that existed at the time. Where the project is now, back then was just a typical central park located in the block, but there was little pressure on the land use. The organizers of the development never thought that this piece of land would be so valuable so they decided to leave it as an open space. It remained so for many years until slowly the park was completely surrounded by all these tall buildings starting with a Mercedes dealer.

The park was underutilized, with people walking their dogs, or the mechanics from the dealer playing football during lunchtime. So a developer comes with the vision of the future, and he is trying to convince the authorities to develop this contested piece of land. The authorities in this case were three distinct entities; the city of Mexico, the local government and an organization of the tenants and owners of buildings in the neighborhood. They decided to grant permission for a commercial venture, so long as it was underground, because the neighborhood was adamant to not allow anything to be built on top of the park. This is just a euphemism because the park was just an undeveloped patch of land really.

The other component of this was there was a huge deficit of car parking spaces, and there was a crisis for many years as a result. So the developer thought "what if I built underground parking and I just ask everyone around to hire my car spaces as a pension," which is like renting the space monthly. It's very clever because he was guaranteed that the funding was there as long as he provided the parking spaces. With 1500 parking spaces the numbers would work.

So there are three components. The first is the parking garage in four levels. Then there is the commercial retail on top of that which is comprised of three levels. Then, of course, on top is the park. So the parking makes sense for the developer, the commercial space is a nice contribution to the community, and the park was the critical condition that was not to be violated.

The developer actually wanted more, so we decided to go for this very daring architecture. It takes the light into the space with this very large atrium that comes into the heart of the retail. The basic concept is how can we translate what is overground to what is underground. The problem was how do we bring both the daylight and park into the retail environment? There was nothing quite like this at the time in Mexico, so as we researched the concept we only found a few examples worldwide, and nothing with this type of program. We wanted to make it feel as though you are in the city and not underground. The solution, and I am being entirely honest about this, is something we came up with ourselves and did not copy anybody because there are so few examples out there. I assume that others would have very similar ideas to ours somewhere in the world because it is so simple. That said, it was difficult to conceptualize but was very easy to sell the idea to the developer. Because he was already happy with the economics of the parking spaces he was very open to try something like this.

As far as issues around sustainability, we take it very seriously because we do not think it should be used just as a marketing tool. Now, it should be compulsory, it is a moral obligation because it is clear what our impact is on the future, so we need to approach architecture in a more intelligent way. The problem is in Mexico the idea of sustainability is very much optional, perhaps you can LEED certify, but that is it. But this is not something that should be optional when you think about money. Since this is the developer's own building, which he will keep for many years, he was very good at asking the right questions. For instance, how much in energy per month will the building use for the next 20 years?

What is often the case here in Mexico is that the owner wants to pay the least in energy bills but they do not necessarily want to go through the bureaucratic LEED certification process. Sometimes that does not make sense for him or her, but they still want to make sure that we incorporate energy efficient design. We insist on incorporating the best engineering practices within our projects, so that either you can use that as a marketing tool, or if you're not interested in marketing you are still putting money in your pocket. In the case of Garden Santa Fe we went through LEED Certification because it was such a marquee project. The developer was very interested in optimizing the project because he wants to market this as the first commercial retail space, here, that is sustainable. So does sustainable mean the LEED processes, or going beyond the rating system, like social sustainability, technical sustainability, or construction and materials sustainability? It has to all be in one package, and we tried to incorporate that in this project.

In a sense it's not that hard because what we have is 16,000 m² of retail space, which is really not that large, and introducing so much daylight and being in the ground saved significant energy. We were even able to hide the air-conditioning intakes which are disguised in the park. But there is a problem because the area is poorly served by public transportation. It's a typical business district which is not being thought

of for employees. If you want to eat, for instance, it is very expensive because all the restaurants are very fashionable. As an example, my office has maybe 50 people, but 40 of them cannot afford restaurants every day. And the same applies for public transportation, perhaps only 15 in the office have a car so the rest really have to struggle to find public transportation just to get to work. This is a typically poorly planned edge city, which is only connected to the main city with three or four main roads, and is not well provided for in terms of public infrastructure. This is very regrettable in a modern city because we keep making the same mistakes, always. So here we have nice buildings, beautiful retail space, a beautiful new development but what about the public infrastructure? In fact we have some clients request that we have meetings before 9 AM or after 7 PM because the traffic is so poor, all the infrastructure is past its capacity.

I did my masters at the London School of Economics in urban planning, and in the early 1990s it was a fanciful topic to explore urban regeneration. The problem was how to attract people back to the cities, and it was a very philosophical question about how to make our cities more livable. One of the first questions was always how do we provide enough infrastructure and public spaces. Garden Santa Fe is a very nice public space, I don't have any doubt in terms of architecture, but on the weekends the space is just dead. Because the surrounding developments are single use, it is not a family area, it is not a walkable area, it is just businesses. Nowadays our obligation

as architects and planners is to provide for the community. This implies that it's for the greater community, not just those with wealth. So here we need places for the 75% of workers to be able to go and eat, for instance. And if you don't have a car, well you have to struggle to come or leave this area. Certainly in the scope of architecture we can only do so much, but also as a planner we need to think about these things. We need to think in terms of creating a community.

This may take time for people to use the space as we hoped. But what is good is that we were able to take the risk and learn from how people respond. Right now it is too new.

So now we are exploring six or seven projects that are incorporating retail in this way. They don't want to put in just typical spaces, so this idea of having air and light coming down is very attractive. What we are doing here is setting a trend to explore the possibilities of building underground. Here in Mexico we use a ratio based on occupancy of the land, and the density of land-use is regulated by the state. So, if you put something underground it is not counted against you when determining the occupancy of the land. Now clients are asking us to put program underground so that they can maximize what they can build above ground. But that space underground still needs to have architectural value, and that means providing light wells, fresh air, nice landscaping like what we have in Garden Santa Fe. 🙴

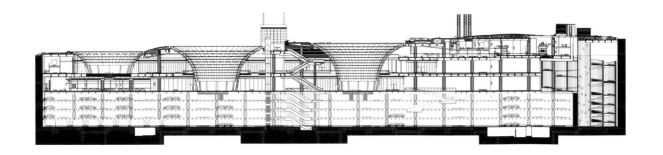

Garden Santa Fe

AUSTRALIA

UNFOLDS]

Sydney-based architect Neil Durbach jokes when talking about Australian architecture, "You know what they say about Australia? It's that thing hanging off the Opera House." Australia found its first true contemporary design language, one that embodies the expression of unfolding, in fact, from two unique Danish visions. The Australian identity of architectural experimentation sits in the lap of architect Jørn Utzon and engineer Ove Arup. The Sydney Opera House has turned architecture into a national form of identity like the Eiffel Tower did for France a century earlier. In anticipation of parametric design, the power of those white tiled kinetic eggshell roofs, endlessly unfurling, has insipred a nation. Underneath their shimmer is an attitude of independence and determination.

Then there is Glenn Murcutt's language of sweeping roofs and swinging walls, which has become an amalgamation of the built and natural environments. His expressive and demi-organic palette shows a way out of the clutches of the imported English Victorian bridle. By making place the priority and digging into his boyhood experiences of growing up in Papua New Guinea's ancient vernacularism, a new, unselfconscious, and dynamic formulation of renewable architecture has bloomed and spread. The unflinching affection of form embracing natural elements has demonstrated the aesthetic benefits of using passive gestures to coax the sun, wind, and water. His work's influence has largely avoided a design culture of mimicry and instead has created a language about the lasting importance of environment in architecture and how design must bow to conditions.

Added to these influences is Australia's prehistoric building vernacular, the humpies of Aborigines, which are the simplest of shelters. Made from bark and branches, they soon dissolve into the landscape as their creators move on. I admire the lightness and humbleness of such shelter, which was used for thousands of years. It is based on the simple and robust idea of use what is around you, nothing more. All of us are ultimately at the whim of the elements, artificially protected by a third skin which can paradoxically burden us as it grows more complex. The lesson from almost every architect in this chapter is that passive measures are what work, not an over reliance on technology.

I find myself coming back to Australian architecture again and again, not because they are the most beautiful buildings, the most technically sophisticated, or necessarily the most sustainable, but because they are bold inquiries. This process is evolving into a contemporary vernacular of kinetic design, not just one of form and function but of attitude. Studio 505's Pixel building's mesmerizing colored wing facade is a clear and unambiguous cry: "I am here, I mean something," and thus has been popularly dubbed the biggest small sustainable building in the world. You're not supposed to like how it looks, but you have to acknowledge that environmental design is an important, perhaps critical value. Instead of reinterpreting its surroundings, it reinvents them. Since the built environment is evolving like no other time in history, those who embrace and catalyze change also reap it rewards.

Heat and drought have always been a part of life in Australia, but the continent is one of the quickest to become adversely affected by global warming. The reality of the cities running out of water in the mid 2000s changed not just infrastructure planning, but beckoned a new social attitude of conservation first. Along with the change in precipitation, unprecedented heat waves are now punishing the landscape unlike anything in recorded history. The cities suffer the most because heat islands wilt conventional buildings and infrastructure. Blackouts are common as air conditioning puts an unmanageable burden on the grid, leaving inhabitants to fend for themselves in buildings not designed to be comfortable without active measures. This ecological toll signals that surviving, and potentially thriving, is directly related to the design of the built environment.

Being on the edge requires a resolute and at times aggressive effort, which creates fertile ground for experimentation and leadership. Understanding Australia's architecture is about accepting the union of opposites. Glenn Murcutt's influence is as a rural architect, but the challenge is urban. The nation is intensely cosmopolitan with 9 out of 10 of its citizens living in an urban area, and yet the national character is deeply independent, self-reliant, with an identity inseparable from the land. Although famously anti-authoritarian, Australians have created sophisticated environmental regulations as well as a suffocating building bureaucracy. Australians love sports and sometimes a good barney is countered by a desire for reflection and the embracing of cultures. After all, almost everyone there is no more than a few generations from being an immigrant. They have no qualms about making generalizations about themselves and then promptly prove the opposite. The result is an English design vernacular of a century earlier standing next to a new, bright and eclectic, built typology.

The mix of complex culture and unique land is fertile for architecture to assertively pursue high performance and reformulate aesthetic values. Unfolding architecture is a fundamental expression of purpose in the form of an articulated gesture, which manifests in multiple formal and conceptual ways: the Commonwealth Place cradles, the Rooftop Penthouse juts, Perforated House liberates the contemporary from the banal, and the Templestowe Reserve Sporting Pavilion kinetically charges an entire space. All of these buildings explore an experimentation that pursues both performance and culture with active design intent, environmentally rooted and expressed as a bold playfulness. It is a fine line as many other projects fall into bland or absurd gestures to please a style or narrow criteria.

Behind the design bluster is a sensitive examination of what performance means in a building. How do traditional means of energy savings and space making, like the veranda, adaptive programming, cross ventilation, thermal massing, and shading, translate to a 21st-century architecture? How does a building respond to place, transform it, and engage in a dialog with the public about its environmental value? Can a culture move beyond status, short-term economics, fashion, and guardedness to embrace new ideas that can sustainability reformulate an entire city? Each project's strength is a very clear formulation of the question of values.

The world we shape through design is a measure of our purpose. I end this book's inquiry with the unassuming Park Bench House by Sean Godsell. He illuminates how we can value our shared environment and become more human by integrating a designed space with the intention of benefiting everyone. As we become more human, we can recognize the nature of ourselves, that which is inseparable from others and from the rhythms of a complex and nurturing environment.

RMIT University is a long-standing liberal arts school with a sprawling urban campus layered in generations of avant-garde architecture in downtown Melbourne. Their growing campus is now flanked by the Design Hub on a high profile corner of the city where the trolley artery and car thorough-fares meet. The multi-use facility merges studios for post-graduate design students, a vast material archive, and ongo-ing exhibitions. At its heart the program is about the process of creativity, so rather than furthering the shock value of pre-vious campus projects, Sean Godsell cooled the palette down, and used the tools of perception to keep the experience con-stantly novel.

The rigorous exterior of sandblasted disks of glass mask the masses proportions, creating a dizzying effect when ap-proached, which can be off-putting at first. The disks pivot through the day like vertical blinds to control interior light and heat gain. With a little bit of time, you will be rewarded as the building slowly reveals it secrets. The rigorous facade changes tempo throughout the day, sometimes a teal grid in direct daylight, then a more delicate steel blue lace revealing the top floor's open-air layout when back lit by the sun. In the evening the floors become fully exposed, introducing the interior grid.

The interior maintains the exterior's vigor, but adds the play of space. As Godsell and his design partner Hayley Franklin walked me through the elongated subterranean labyrinth, perversely tight corridors, tall doors, and along the plotted meeting rooms on the roof deck, I found myself constantly chuckling at the unexpectedness of it all. These are ideal con-ditions for the creative process to evolve.

ARCHITECT
SEAN GODSELL ARCHITECTS
MELBOURNE, AUSTRALIA
2012
13,000 SQUARE METERS

[RMIT DESIGN HUB]

SEAN GODSELL

"There's a lot of junk out there that is parading as architecture in the name of sustainability. They are people with a really loud drum saying I got a double platinum LEED rating building, therefore it must be good. You look at the building and it fails on so many other fronts that it couldn't possibly be accused of being architecture, but there it is. There's always a groundswell now and the groundswell is fast. Things used to manifest slowly, now they peak quickly and it drops away almost as quickly. Of course, architects tend to be more scientific than that, so I think of it is all the building science that we are taught at the university is putting that into practice in a creative way. Most good architects have been environmentally attuned for a lot longer than when it became an issue.

I was happy to take risks for environmental design before it became fashionable to talk about it. We knew about global warming in the early 1990s, but it wasn't mainstream. Then I just talked about it as a way of making things. In my case it was an interest in the local conditions and finding a response that was cost efficient. I started my practice on the smell of an oily rag, doing really low-budget work, so the first time I was looking at resources like recycled material was out of necessity to get projects over the line. The first buildings where all these things came together was my own house called the Kew House where I am still living. In that building there is recycled timber, a passive cooling system, shading system, rainwater harvesting, and soon there will be solar, so it's a building that will continue to evolve. That was in the mid 1990s. Incorporating these elements like an operable shading device was the first one I've tried, but it evolved quite quickly into a shade skin so that we could still get glass buildings but protect the glass. The main issue in a temperate climate like Melbourne is keeping the heat out. A decade or so later we start talking about environmental design and then legislating for it. When we started making it compulsory for houses to have energy ratings and so forth. Everyone had to jump on board and then it became mainstream. That's okay because architecture should be ahead of the game.

Can I be more playful and daring with my architecture? The answer to the question is yes, if you have a client and a budget, you can afford to experiment. The RMIT Design Hub came out of a project that I did in Arizona right down near the Mexican border. I had a San Francisco based client who wanted to do an echo resort in the desert. The design for the cabins was the first time I did a solar skin that had collectors in it. The Arizona project died a slow death; we were absolutely killed at the planning phase because local residents did not want to see it happen. The client simply had to stop but the idea didn't stop.

The idea is a building skin emulating a human skin, exploring how human skin performs a number of functions. We wanted the building in Arizona to sweat like human sweat to keep it cool because it was in a high desert. If you have air movement through the building it would cool itself through the façade. What the RMIT Design Hub did is turned it into an operable shade skin that has the potential for, and is plumbed for but is not doing it at the moment, a facade that sweats. We have air intakes at the perimeter grille, which means that air can move over a membrane that is wetted by harvested rainwater so we can bring cool fresh air into the building. Now we do not have the need for artificial cooling during summer. RMIT was keen on that, but, when it came to solar photovoltaics we said you have huge capital costs for the infrastructure and little power back in fact. We cannot justify it, so why don't we be more radical and build a building that has the potential to evolve not only over years, but decades. We will make this kind of beautiful skin that is cellular in appearance and put in the infrastructure to be adapted. At RMIT you have an environmental design group and a solar energy group that talks industry, so why don't you get those people experimenting on it.

We were given the task to find a way to make the entire building adaptable. So we said, "Instead of designing buildings for you, if you're going to buy a building what would you buy?" Straightaway they said they would buy a warehouse and used furniture. So the research floors in the building are called warehouses, and we designed a whole set of furniture for them all on wheels. We then said, okay, you're an intelligent user, we don't have to prescribe a way to live in this building. If you go to the computer gaming floor now it's really nice. It is completely full of crap, but it is good stuff—they are hanging plants from the ceiling, they made it their own space. In practice, that's the idea of the building designed for chaos.

They have a big publicly accessible exhibition program now, which they have never had. Kids making facade models for a building can make full-scale models like robotics shop in the building, that sort of thing. That gives it a public face and puts design on the agenda, that means politicians start sniffing, and here's a growth industry we are supporting through this institution.

To understand the impact of the building on that prominent site you have to understand its context. What we have earmarked immediately to the west of the building is an 80-story tower, and immediately to the north a 30-story tower, neither owned by RMIT. I felt that this building needed to claim the corner and occupy it. Melbourne is a gridiron like Chicago and New York, and has big avenues that link the south to the north. That is a very powerful corner, though they had to be very conscious of doing with what was to come. People sometimes get kind of concerned that it's too rigorous, but when the rest of the site is developed, you become quite a strong little bookend to a more complex and larger development.

The forecourt between the archive and the Hub in the end becomes a thruway, a pedestrian theater into to the rest of the site. We're taking about 10% of the site in that building. Then there is a secondary path that runs east to west, which is alleyway. The thing about the facade hitting the street the way it does is all about that, it is to be strong. It's almost a landscape, not a building when you imagine in the context of an 80-story building. It will become almost like a gatepost into that development. The building is a deliberate play of scale. I removed all the tectonic elements that we would associate with the building, so the things that give perception of scale are gone.

I stuck one element back in. The main entry I stole from Michelangelo and played with what he designed for the San Lorenzo Basilica in Florence. He puts a door within a door so that the doorway is actually

double height. It completely distorts your perception of the scale of the building as you approach it from the south. And when you get to the doorway, its massive, a 5.5-meter-high space that is nearly two and a half stories high. It denies you knowledge of the size of the thing until you go inside it.

You never want buildings to get predictable. You don't want people to get bored with the thing or understanding of it to the point where they don't want to go in. That would be a disaster, so it's deliberately playful. Informed users should have that playfulness, it should tease you and draw you through it. Once you are enticed in, you just want to keep going. At the entry of the Design Hub is a little slice like a peephole where you can look down to the level below which is a public exhibition space. It's like a peeping tom window on the sidewalk where you can stand and look into the building to just get a hint what is going on. You add the fact that most of the building denies you visual access, then that should be enough if you have any creative juice in your body.

The next thing once you start thinking "I feel brave and courageous and interested" is you end up on a triple helix of circulation so you can start that journey and you can literally be drawn a certain way, and as you go you can see people going in other directions and can't get to them. Or you'll need to know the way of cheating that route to get to them. That's playing with childhood memory, and a lot of architecture is about that creating of excitement. So these buildings are about the journey, denial and the reward of finding. A lot of my houses have that kind of protraction, you don't just figure it out, you actually have to work it.

Circulation is important. In the last few houses it's about how spaces are divided based on Eastern cultures. The Design Hub is the first building in four or five years where I used the section consciously by compressing and releasing. The houses that predated that building had taken the section out of the debate, and they use the division of space, which is a Japanese technique to make drama. They take the corridor out as much as possible, different spaces divided by sliding walls.

I spent a lot of time in Japan and it's always been a fundamental influence. The stair in the Design Hub is a tribute to Kazuo Shinohara's phase of what he called *sliced spaces*. So the Japanese manipulate space beautifully, and draw on that thousand-year-old culture of the Ise Shrine and Katsura Imperial Palace, then they can bring in everything that the West brings to make a complex mix.

The Design Hub is the first time in ages that I use the Western tricks I learned as an undergraduate. I drop the ceiling low onto your head and then release it to create drama. I kind of abandoned that for a while when I was building the practice because I felt that everyone was doing that, so I wanted to try to make space without doing it. When the Japanese do that they do it in very tight circumstances in very clever ways. What they do, which is the point of departure, is that they make spaces that are fundamentally impractical. That sort of largeness and small buildings is remarkable.

My buildings are animated. The reasons are twofold, in the wintertime the buildings have different requirements than in the summertime, so that's a good thing. But it's also to animate simple form, to make simple form more complex. They can't be dumb boxes, they have to be complex boxes. The trick is to put the formal elements as a functional one. Each project is a one-off and maybe I need another trick. We are a very funny office in that I sit and do all the window details still. We don't buy the package, we specify how we want the window. People ask how on Earth we get to do that from scratch each time. But, each time we evolve details like a thermal break in a mullion where a male and female piece come together but are separated by neoprene or polystyrene. If you want your building to perform better and pay less for power and gas here's a way of doing it. It's not only practical but it looks good. Passive is very important but also has to be architecture. You can't remove the architecture from passive design.

I have to be able to rationalize the design decision. I am fundamentally a rationalist. If I can't find a reason for doing something I can't actually do it. We have a commission at the moment to do a pavilion in a garden and it took three really advanced schemes to be rejected before we found one that works. The one that works is completely rational, a response to things like security, vandalism and graffiti, and things like that as well as being architectural. You can have great ideas that are completely capricious. There are buildings around the city with heavily animated profile façades for example that pay no heed to orientation. There's a lot of shape making taking precedence over practical matters. Trouble with that is when decisions are made, shape making for its own sake costs money and deprives the project of funding that could improve

its performance. In that sense the Design Hub is one of very few examples where you incorporate the two, where the performance then becomes the architecture.

When it comes to incorporating "environmental" features in a building you can't make a cliché out of it. The architecture has to be serious about this as well; it cannot be about separate issues, it has to be about the same issue. If that make sense it's about just assuming it will have all of that in an intelligent way rather than a "hey look at me" way.

I am always the odd guy out here. My work is completely different from everyone else's. There is a lot of shock jock architecture in Melbourne. I am ambivalent in a sense about Melbourne's architecture. There was a sensational documentary on television a few weeks ago about the Apollo 11 landing on the on the Moon in which everything went wrong and they still pull it off. Armstrong and Aldrin were just going by the seat-of-their-pants. A scientist being interviewed said nowadays with risk management we would have never been allowed to take off let alone try to land. I thought to myself yep, that's the world we live in. Risk taking is now the anathema to architecture. Yet you have to take risk to do architecture.

I became punch drunk with the Design Hub. We were fighting so many fights all at once to get the risk managers out of the way and get them to see reason. Of course we have to respect people with disabilities and design for them but at one point I said why don't we just cover the whole building in tactile indicators and take out what we don't need because that's going be a lot quicker. We had tactile indicators everywhere.

So yes, it's a good place and not a good place to work. The opportunities in Australia are better than anywhere else in the world. We have no fear building but we also then control. When you do that in Australia you are told very quickly, "Now you can't do this or that." So we have this problem, but Melbourne is a city that at least purports to encourage design. That's good and I support that.

As far as the future of the environment, I believe that humans will get things right and will fix the problems. The doomsayers are saying this century will be it, and science supports that worst-case scenario. If we are on top of the food chain we're there for a reason because we are intelligent enough to define problems and solve them. So we can make things better again if we do them wrong the first time. In India I was giving a talk about a month ago and I said architects are not politicians. We don't control the purse strings, all we can do is lead by example. So you'd hope that we are seeing things and responding. 🙿

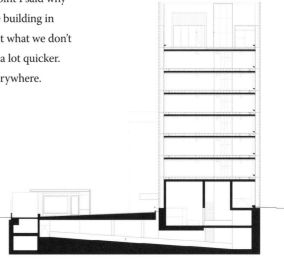

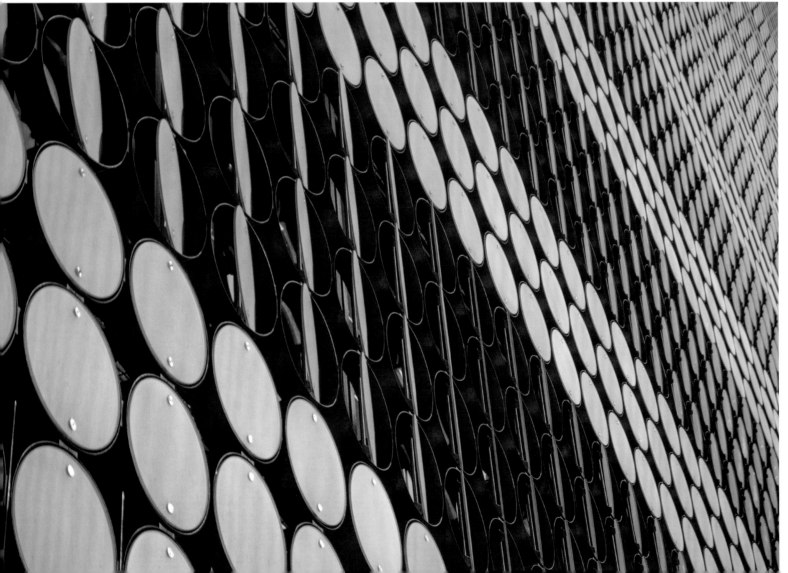

Earl Carter

ARCHITECT
FRANCIS-JONES MOREHEN THORP
SURRY HILLS, SYDNEY, AUSTRALIA
2009
2,497 SQUARE METERS

[SURRY HILLS LIBRARY & COMMUNITY CENTRE]

With a lively street scene littered with boutiques, bars, and beauty salons the textured Surry Hills neighborhood is about immersion with the upwardly mobile set. Tasteful but edgy, high performance, and accessible, the Surry Hills Library and Community Centre engages the complexity of various public programs and opens to the street like an unclasped jewel box. That is the first order of business, to be refined but transparent, by coolly reflecting a bluegreen gaze onto the small simple grass plot where countless strollers enjoy an ice cream and conversation before their next encounter.

At the street level and below is a small library and resource center. Above a community center and offices, topped with a children's daycare. This means many daily visitors and a substantial need for cooling. That begins with the automated two-story wooden louvers to the east side facing the street which control the solar gain through the course of a sunny morning. The southern glass prism atrium, the building's most notable feat of engineering, is the visual center and also functions as the main air exchange. The outer layer captures fresh air from the rooftop and distributes it to an underground labyrinth where it is naturally conditioned by the earth. It is then chilled via a ground source heat pump and introduced to the interior's multiple floors via the interior portion of the atrium. It is elaborate but effective at reducing the energy needed to keep occupants comfortable.

The roof is capped with a PV array, green roof, and open-air play area for the daycare center. Between multiple programs, and a clear fusion of design, performance and technology, the building is as dense as it is approachable.

ANDREW MAYNARD | MARK AUSTIN

AM: I think we went through the modernist stage when everyone was saying, "Hooray, machines for living in." Energy and technology will move us forward so why bother with eaves, just air condition the hell out of. It was like that for a couple of generations and it's like we've had to relearn the fundamentals. Because the vast majority of the work we do is working with older buildings, it's really interesting to peel away the layers and discover how things were put together. You go into these old warehouses, which have been cut up with varying degrees of sensitivity: some are just savage tiny little boxes, while other ones keep this amazing structure going. It's interesting looking at the disassembling of a building. It is a great way to learn about tectonics, and how a previous generation put something together.

With older buildings I try to sit structures next to each other rather than have a tumor growing out. The new object represents now next to an older object, and we go fit it out in a way where we try to revere it in a very respectful way instead of applying too much to it. With House House we make a very clear distinction on the outside, but on the inside it works really well because you can tell what is old and what is introduced. It means that with the layering you can tell this is new and that is the inherited building on the other side.

We often refer to Japanese architecture, which I really love because of the idea that we have such an abundance of space. It is the idea of importing an architecture that is so confined by place like Tokyo or elsewhere in Japan. We say, well what if we did that and we actually sow some discipline?

People think that we are anti-suburb but I don't think I am. I think I am critical of suburbs. Everyone sees the suburb-eating robot thinking what I'm doing is attacking them, it's not really about that. It's about recognizing where suburbs came from, fundamentally the result of the car and moving away from cities, which were seen as hostile. But it's really a reaction to what was seen as one of the biggest threats Peak Oil, which unfortunately, depending on your perspective, hasn't come to be. I think the comment on the suburb was really that it is unsustainable. But architecture is only a tiny percentage of this so it doesn't help to say bugger off, we only work here. That is not very useful.

MA: Our work shows what you can do as infill architecture in tight spaces. You can create very quality spaces vertically. Melbourne has a lot of leftover space, as a lot of cities have, and you can slowly piecemeal quality spaces internally and create a lot more density.

AM: That's why we always had a lot of problems with the whole prefab notion that we looked into. Many of the blocks are a dissimilar width. If you have a 5-meter block somebody else has a 5.2-meter block and you try to put in something prefab into that you lose that space. Again, you have a problem with what you'd do in the city translating to the suburbs.

As far as designing interiors we just try to do simple things where possible, like not cut across spaces. You have to be really economical about the space, so as soon as you cut across the space you make it very difficult to deal with. Victorian houses are notorious for it around here. You'll have a whole leg past a couple of bedrooms and crank and go across a living space. Something like Hill House was really difficult because we were stubbornly trying to put the new building on the back boundary. With the new building and the old building to achieve a bright sunny courtyard in the middle really forced us to be unconventional with the circulation.

The great thing is that it's easy to convince clients to try these little ideas. Now we are doing a few houses that are of some size so the clients just naturally want more. We plead, "Why don't we just leave it small and do that great gesture?" They respond, "Yeah, but let's just make it bigger." They're quite shocked when we say let's not do that, how much do you need?

MA: We just had two days of meetings with clients and it's the same thing.

AM: I think it's cultural, they go, "Why do that to us?" Well, you end up with a better quality space, better connection to the outside, more outdoor space. We have all this, so why not go as horizontal as you want. We're also a very aspirational society, people are thinking about coming to visit them in their house. So often they talk about it being like a stage set.

MA: They are thinking about Christmas day and not every day.

AM: If it's Christmas day, spend the day outside in the sun, it's summer here.

We refer to Japanese work a lot, but there are a couple of things that are very different. Legislation is different so they can just build. We spent so much time trying to figure out how to make handrails disappear or give them a secondary function. We are constantly having to push our buildings, which is difficult on a small site. Also, the litigious nature of things here, we

have to take so many responsibilities. A British architect that I've spoken with who works in Japan said as soon as the builder takes the documents everything is their responsibility. And that's why you see such amazing quality work.

MA: Good architecture has always been difficult. You can take the easy path and you'll see the results. If we kept doing the same thing over and over again it wouldn't be any fun.

AM: Our responsibility to the clients is to get all that passive stuff right. Most people are surprised to hear that we almost never specified solar panels. It's like, "Hang on, you guys are supposed to do sustainable stuff," but why pay us much or the builder much, we can just call the solar company. If we're pitching that as if you need an architect to spec solar to make a sustainable house, then we are lying. You need us to get the eaves right, something as simple as that. Sun control has always been big here, maybe not this far south, but New South Wales upwards it's all about the veranda. The vernacular is the veranda and that's been held onto quite a lot. Clients do not necessarily get it a lot of times, they liked the look of the vernacular but fundamentally it's functional and spatial. So, if we take those reasons, say great, and put it in there it does not necessarily have to be executed or look the same way. Fundamentally that is what the Butler House is, where a couple had two young boys, though they had to abandon this place and move out to the suburbs. We thought we could knock the roof off and put the backyard on there and get a view of the sea. Where we went in cut off the roof, three or four other units the put a deck on top of

the roof. But nobody is up on those decks because it's so exposed. Another reason why we cut up the roof was to make the deck closer to the living space. You need interaction between the levels, which is something we're always trying to do. If you break up spaces then you might as well use a mobile phone. With things like the louvered wall you can just open up and talk downstairs. The first thing the client said was with two boys growing up they needed to break the sound so they wanted glass around the staircase. We really didn't want to do that so we proposed to try new things. We installed louvers to control the sound, and on the other side using shelves, carpet, and knickknacks was a way we approached it softly, designing around the problem. It all works nicely.

We both have young kids. You know, no matter how great we make the bedroom they always want to be with you. They will grab their whole mess and bring it to you, so we love the idea of sliding walls so they can see you leave it there or make it into a room, sweep everything back into it. We designed a house that we call the Toy Management House (Black House). It's an existing building where we built up the floor 400 millimeters, which is seat height, and the entire floor in the living space is basically a big toy box. If the kid wants the toys, open up the floor and they get to play in it. For the parents gravity is on their side so they can sweep everything in and close it.

Every project is really hard. A client will ask for us to show them an idea and we will show them one, but we will probably do 10 or 12 that are rubbish.

MA: They are fun to do at the time. You wake up in the morning look at it with fresh

eyes, but I don't find it to be a struggle.

AM: I do find the design process really painful. I wake up in the morning muttering, "How do you do this again?" I might feel lost thinking that the ones that we did really well were flukes and I got nothing. Over the years I found the only way was to just keep on going, keep on going. And then I find little bits and then it's necessary to get everyone involved and tell them what I'm thinking. When something I'm not sure about gets kicked around, it either will be canned or they will explain why it's working. And in that is the whole project and all the other stuff gets pushed out.

MA: And that's the hard thing to do, to find the one kernel that everything evolves from. All the things we describe can click together.

AM: It's a jigsaw, but a jigsaw made up of lots of other jigsaws. Like it's never going to be put together completely.

MA: Designing for the day-to-day level, we're talking about larger houses and larger living areas, is their idea of entertaining for a very small percentage time. It's designing three or four people to live in that house. The needs of those people in terms of what the room does, that's when you have to start working through all these ideas.

AM: And everything has to have a reason and we jettison ideas really quickly. Like with House House, even though it has a reason, which is abstract, if it's not practical then at the end of the day we will not use it. At the end of the day, it didn't stop the stereotype of the house's idea, but if we're going to put timber on the building we had to consider the graffiti that is so prevalent

around here. If someone comes by and tags it, how do we manage that process? If there is that joy and fun on one level but it does not have purpose, we will get rid of that. We're trying desperately for it not to look like a sustainable building because that should not be aestheticized.

It's so much easier to build a McMansion with solar panels to get to the Green Star building process than to say we haven't done any sustainable things here but we've managed to make it small and well-connected. Anglesea Beach House is a good example of that, as the owner was asking do we extend this thing or do we knock it down and do some super duper green house. The whole time we were against knocking it down because of the carbon of what's there—to put in a big glass box and air condition the hell out of it would probably be way ahead than if we put in the greenest new building and then spent 50 years paying off what we used in materials.

In the process of working on a smaller budget and being paid less we are working with the ethic to say we want to make a profit and do it the right way. Our smaller buildings are almost double the cost per square meter, out in the suburbs people think we are crazy for what we spend. We build something small and quite brilliant, at least hopefully it will be. 🙶

Fraser Marsden

AMA

Fraser Marsden

Fraser Marsden

Peter Bennetts

Peter Bennetts

Peter Bennetts

AMA

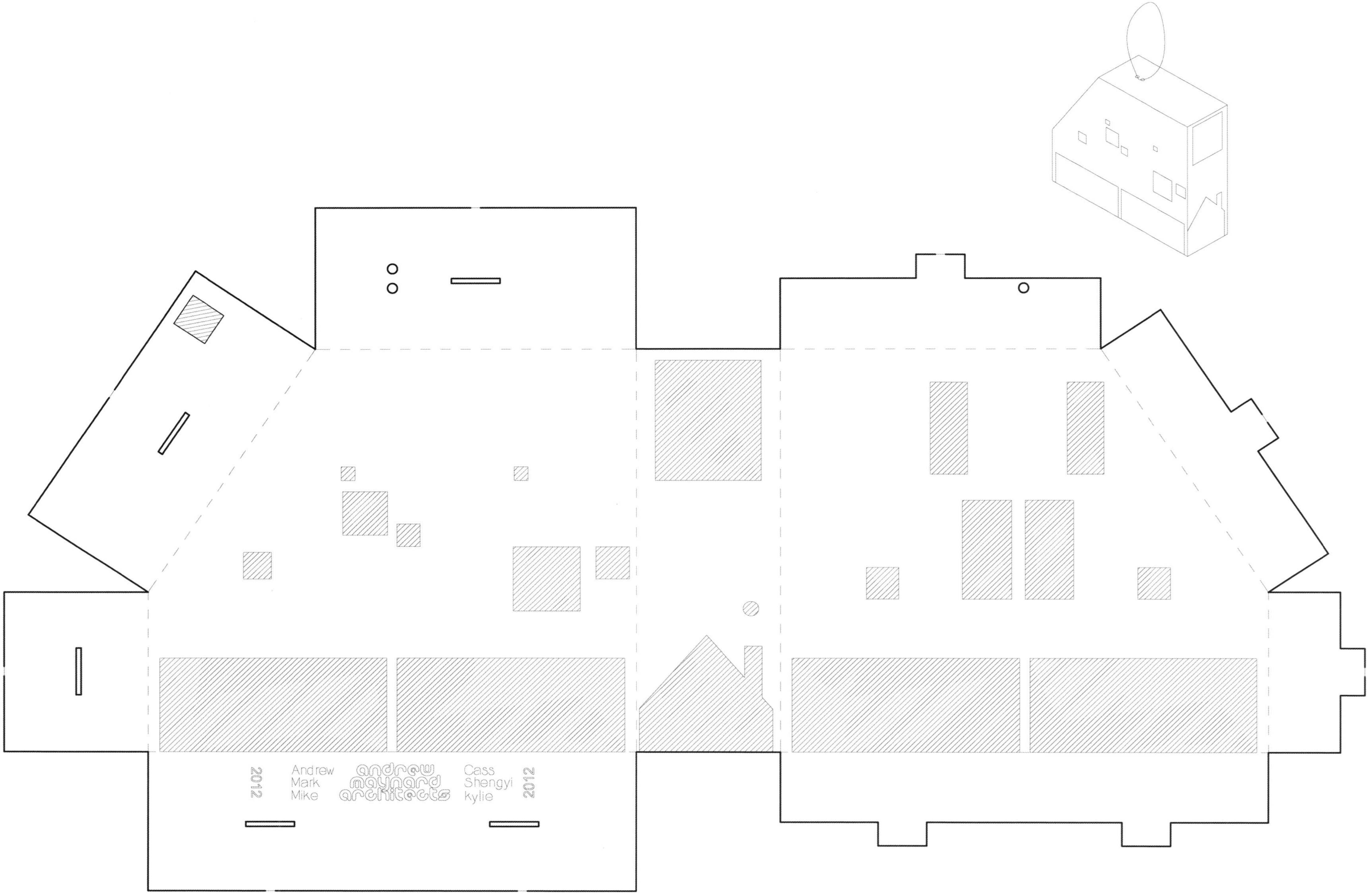

Andrew
Mark
Mike

Cass
Shengyi
kylie

andrew maynard architects

2012

2012

ARCHITECT
MHN DESIGN UNION
BONDI, SYDNEY, AUSTRALIA
2010
180 SQUARE METERS

[ROOFTOP PENTHOUSE]

Facing one of the great tourist beaches of the world, a rather plain and decrepit Art Deco apartment block has been revitalized by an unlikely set of circumstances. A futuristic penthouse, rising from the pale blue stucco host, gains fresh living space in the highly sought neighborhood. The project adds much needed density where it is most often ignored by inserting it on top of, rather than supplanting, the existing neighborhood. Call it "symbiotic architecture" or "parasitic design" the process claims existing, often decrepit buildings to add new functions in an established neighborhood. The low weight prefabricated materials demonstrates the capacity of contemporary construction systems to integrate around existing infrastructure with minimal interruption to the street life.

Since the technical hurdles of structure and egress aligned so well, the architects could explore opportunities in the angular instincts of the project to express its distinct break from the past. Tucking it away from the street-side parapet adds an outdoor space seamlessly integrating with the interior an angular sliding glass wall. That angularity is expressed throughout its interior and exterior.

While the choice in materiality is not necessarily high in thermal performance, the home takes full advantage of the prevailing cooling breezes caught by an integrated water element. The unrelenting white echoes natural light deep into the living spaces.

" Our original offices were almost next door to the Rooftop Penthouse in Bondi. It's one of those projects that you get spoiled on; if there is a question or issue I just pop on down, it was a three-minute walk. Out of the office window I could see the project built on the roof. The project was for a client that we had done quite a bit of work for previously. It was an apartment building with a three-story walk-up and very basic, with shops on the first floor levels and apartments above. The client lived in one of those apartments with his young family. This is a true story. He was told by his wife to find somewhere to dry his clothes because there were no balconies and they were sick of using the dryer. He went up to the rooftop and luckily enough it was a flat roof, no equipment was up there. Imagine this 250 square meter plate of prime real estate opposite the beach and he thought this would be a great place to put in a penthouse.

So, he approached the building committee and said he would like to purchase an option on that roof space. It was a win-win situation in that the money that was given to the committee will be put right back into the upkeep of the building. The building was in need of an upgrade, the lobby was dilapidated and the owners have all been living there for a long time. Bondi never used to be this trendy place, it's only caught on in the last 30 or 40 years. Those apartments are pretty old and beat up, so the building's condition didn't really match the property value of the area. So, the money my client is bringing in made a lot of sense to revitalize the entire building in terms of the lobby, facade treatments, new awnings. After this project, we have gotten

many inquiries to do something similar with other buildings where they wanted to reclaim the roof space.

Our client on this particular project is a builder himself, and we've done many projects together before, so this project was a little different in that the client would also be the builder. On this particular project, a lot of stars had to be aligned for it to happen. The first hurdle was to get the approval of the building committee. Second, because it's on the main street, Bondi has quite a bit of heritage significance so the council is quite careful as to what they are willing to approve, and although the building itself is not heritage listed it is a part of the character of the street. For us to put a modern building on top was a gamble. There other projects where one or two stories have been put on top of an existing building, but they've always mimicked the existing details. Strangely, it was quite a smooth process going through council, the neighbor's reaction was very good. The council's main comment was that they didn't want to see the building. So we thought, cool, we will make it white and it will just blend in. We actually pushed the building further back to create a roof terrace because being just opposite Bondi beach it is pretty ideal. Even though you can't see it from the front, it does have a very strong northerly profile. Bondi does get a bit rowdy, but all you can hear on the roof are the buses on the street. Having said that, people choose to live in this part of Bondi, they want to be a part of it. There are only a couple other places here that have this type of space.

As far as the design itself, when he came to us with it, it seemed like one of those

low-key projects, and we knocked down our fees because it was such a small project. We very quickly realized that we had something exciting. It was one the situations where we have constraints that make the project more interesting than "Here's a massive piece of land, put a house on there." I still remember that I was busy and actually gave it to one of the student staff to work on, and then he did something that was sculptural, so I thought let's just do something really crazy here guys. We wanted to demarcate ourselves from the building, which is quite rectangular, so we are going to do something a bit more angular to emphasize something between the new and old. Anything new was on an angle and that permeated through the whole of the building.

At first we were thinking of doing something in Corten steel, but that would've really scared them off. We used a high-gloss product. It's durable and hard-wearing and the client uses this product, so it's a way of showing it off. Since it's an angular building, why not clad it with joints there, also at an angle. It was one of those rare projects where architect and contractor really worked well together because every panel had to be site measured. Even though budget was not a primary concern, with this project I wanted to really reduce any waste materials. We worked out a process of turning sheet goods, maximizing what we can use on the facade.

Usually apartments these days are built so that most of the space is given to the apartments and very minimal space is left for the lobbies, which is termed dead space because you can't sell it. This building was built in the 1920s and luckily the top floor has an alcove, just leftover space. We needed to provide stair access obviously for egress and fire exits. That was the best place for a spiral stair. If he didn't have that space he would've had to buy someone's unit for the project or it wouldn't happen. That stairway generated the whole layout. Since the stairs are in the middle we could put the living space to where the views are.

The other aspect to its design is it had to be a lightweight structure. The existing structure was masonry walls, concrete slabs, and again as luck would have it, they built, for some reason, these very thick external walls, which are not commonplace. We wanted to lift the building as high as possible off the roof so the parapet in the front does not block the view. That also provided us a place for services underneath. This idea of a lightweight building again pointed us to the idea of being angular and slight. The building is primarily steel framing and finished inside with a firebreak. Access was a big issue because we could not have any trucks on the street, so we had to use the sideline, which was also heavily used. From memory, that was only once a week, so they had to program what they would bring up to the site and what they would bring down. We had to take shop drawings to a fabricator who created a 3-D model and then made the frame off-site.

The building was like an erector set quite literally, they had an instruction set like an IKEA furniture instruction sheet. I told you how I could see the site from my window. The foreman calls and tells me the spiral staircase is going in. I like to take credit for it but it was actually an accident, I designed a circular skylight above the stairs but never did I think that I would use that skylight to

drop the stairs through. So they are able to crane the stairs through the skylight and into the hole of the existing roof. If that didn't work we would have been screwed.

The other thing we experimented with is using angled sliding doors. We've done angled glass many times, but never doors at an angle, there are very few examples in Australia. We also wanted to extend the inside to the outside. We have a water feature on the outside that we wanted to bring into the house. The idea was that we want to bring cool breezes into the house but didn't want to see the building next door. So we put in these low-level louvers that pull in cooled air that goes over the water feature as well as light on the south side. Inside, that water feature is covered in glass.

I like to tell him that he stole that land. The real beauty is someone coming up with that idea of offering up money for that space and that money is reinvested into their own building. The existing building would've just crumbled if it wasn't for this project. It would never have been allowed to be knocked down, yet it's not valuable enough to put a lot of money into. It takes a lot of people to do something like this and we are a small part, this was the result of hard work in collaboration. Very rarely do I describe a building as being joyful to build, but this is one of them. When you eliminate money you also eliminate a lot of conflict, and I really didn't charge for all the time I spent in the design phase and during construction so he got a lot of value. As an architect you have maybe a couple projects like this. To sum up the project, everything was a design response for problems that came up, and the product is a result of that. 🙰

MHNDUnion

MHNDUnion

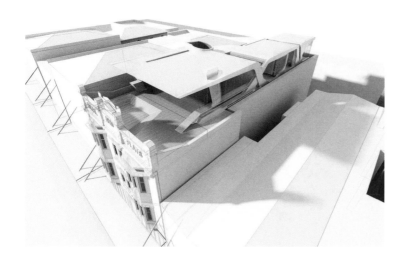

The much sought after Victorian flat is a peculiar English transplant, which while informing cultural ties is distinctly devoid of climate appropriate design, with a typically dark and closed interior and formal facade. Perhaps no other project in this book better articulates and openly challenges vernacularism than Perforated House. Designed for the architect's young family in a classic Victorian neighborhood just north of downtown Melbourne, the project is as much a provocative gesture as a adaptable home.

This little house seems to wink at passersby. By lightly sketching the neighboring ornate century-plus-old vernacular onto an unrepentant austere facade, KUD articulately questions the process of taste. Perforated House cleanses the palette by using light, layered elements. to create a transformative airy living condition. By maximizing a tiny lot with a highly adaptable program and masterful shutter facade the home provides multiple uses through light and movement to adapt to the user needs and the quality of day.

The spirit of the design is an inquiry, as much intellectual as practical, to the nature of what we value in our built environments and how to move more rapidly into adopting climate adaptive building.

ARCHITECT
KAVELLARIS URBAN DESIGN
MELBOURNE, AUSTRALIA
2009
80 SQUARE METERS

[PERFORATED HOUSE]

BILLY KAVELLARIS

"The Perforated House is a litmus test, a real big experiment. It was a project evolved over a number of years as a collective thinking process for us. There's a lot of talk about architecture and its role in this country, what it should be and the influences we have from Europe and America. There's this discussion about regionalism, the Australian vernacular. This country's only a couple of hundred years old, so historically we are babies. We were founded by English settlers, so a lot of what we do here is linked to their architecture and maybe culture, it is European by nature. So the discussion became, why do we have all these Victorian terraced houses, are they appropriate for an Australian landscape? And this discourse shifted towards a perception around the world that we are Crocodile Dundee and we ride kangaroos and we are all farmers. But I think, as you'll discover, we are very cosmopolitan, urbanized, and in many places cutting-edge in what we do.

For KUD, we decided we design for place, environment, and for clients. I think in particular for Melbourne and Sydney a real strength in architecture is a strongly intellectual approach. We talk about the vernacular not in the sense of a rusty shed in the bush. A lot of our work is based on that thinking process, but has moved on. It has evolved because our practice of architecture has a process in that what directly influences us is not really about architectural elements or tectonics, it is really about cultural things. I'm in the process of writing my own book based on the things that make architecture, which in turn makes cities. The things that make the cities are that people built them for other people. I traveled the world quite a bit, and whatever city it may be, if there's a strong architectural flavor then its people

represent it. People are the ones who actually make the city—culture precedes architecture. In our practice we seek to find things that make culture, the idiosyncrasies, shall we say.

Understanding your place is critical. We've done some work internationally, and one of things that is important to understand is exactly the place and the culture you're designing for. You will find Rem Koolhaas is highly critical of this issue. He talks about how Dubai or China has absorbed the Western idea of building the icon manifested in architecture. The French architect designing French buildings in China. Given how the world is accessible immediately, your phone or TV or traveling, it is now becoming a big problem for architecture. There is a lot of criticism around the world from leading architects about this, and I subscribed to this point of view.

All we're saying is you need to be completely aware of where you are, the environment, the culture, the place, all of those things are important to architecture. The story of making places is a lot more complicated than just architecture. The Perforated House is specifically about that. Melbourne is obsessed with the terraced Victorian home. They are more obsessed with the romanticization of it, categorically nostalgic for an English typology shall we say. What usually happens is that we would buy these things and recognize very quickly that they are poorly designed, have poor circulation, poor sustainable outcomes. We gut them, remodel them and then put a new thing in the back to connect with the outside world, a poor model to start building houses. In a country this big and yet the terraced house gives no regard to orientation, or the public realm, or regard to good light. All it is is

big heavy elements with a lot of decoration. We have what's called heritage consultants who say this is an important aspect of our culture and our place and therefore they should be preserved. We agree, but by doing this with new buildings the culture is being diluted.

The Perforated House is basically a critique on that whole idea. So, we sought to raise discussion and provoke people into making a decision by looking at this building and forming their own critique. I would say the overwhelming majority of people responded to this house positively. It's been very well received internationally; and there are those who have very strong views of the building, they hate it. I'm comfortable with both those views provided the people can formulate an opinion and not to sit on the fence and say it's a house. We want to talk about a lot of things that relate to our culture, demography, asking should we really be building big houses in the city typology. Where is the role of urban space, the role of history and what that means to us, should we redefine it? I have a big problem with this so-called sustainable architecture becoming the new fad. Our focus should be on producing really sustainable buildings and not producing images of green stuff in the city.

The Perforated House has three skins: the perforated metal, the glass, and a curtain behind it that runs two stories. A terraced house is usually a dense, heavy, static, fortress sort of thing. The Perforated House is the opposite of that, although it can represent a heavy blunt object if you want. With Perforated House you find that the northern interface is where the open spaces are. The key, I suppose, to responding to the environmental issues is that the Perforated House essentially becomes an outdoor environment. With the glass doors on the north and wall on the perforated south open it becomes an external space. We're interested that the house is not static, so there are many movable parts that change the environment at will. You have to remember that this is a very tight space—the lot is only 75 square meters.

When you open up the walls of the Perforated House you invite the street in. One of the important components of our project is that part of the architecture is its environment or context. For example, the street, in all its glory, was part of our architectural response, and that is an important element to the inside space. So the street itself is a borrowed amenity, a borrowed piece of architecture that we are using for our response. The discussion about public and private space is a huge one.

The mural on the northern wall, the interface where you have the open space, is about this critique on the suburban backyard, the Australian dream. We employed an artist and worked with them but did not give them strict criteria. All we said was we wanted them to represent the daydream or the memory of the Australian backyard and reinterpret in a way that is playful.

Here we have a long planning process and we give the community a say. Planning has become a real science here, it really informs what we do, and is a real political issue for us that affects architectural outcomes. Sometimes it is politically motivated and not what's best for the community. It is not about the benchmark of somebody saying well, "this is the street and this is how it is to be represented." I think that the discussions should be more compelling than that. After Perforated House was built it was great because people would be calling asking to use this as a precedent for reference for other streets in Melbourne where we have this historical context. For new building what is its role? Should it replicate what's there or should it be doing other things.

Whether you like it or not is not what's important. If we're appealing to taste then we are doomed. The house is successful because it provoked a response, discussion, and debate. The irony is our biggest project is $100 million tower and this little house has created much more discussion.

Although we moved on because we've had another child, when we lived there it was great. It was very flexible, had a very small footprint, and the idea was that in an urban context you use the local amenities in your community, such as parks, libraries, whatever it may be. They become your backyard. The idea is when we designed this there's no parking on the lot, there is a park down the street, a train station at the doorstep, and a shopping district close by. It's a critique of these McMansions in suburbs where there are these enormous houses 50 kilometers from the city center. It is the Australian dream where you should have this big block of land and a theater room, five bedrooms, and I'm sure this is a trend in the Western world. If we are going to talk about sustainability that is clearly an unsustainable approach, it's a consumerist approach, and it produces, generally speaking, poor architectural outcomes. The homes become hermit like.

People and cities are not linear, we do not think in linear ways, we do not build in linear ways and problems are never linear, you can never bounce off one then six off another, they are always happening simultaneously. For example, the heritage idea, or the historical component of the site, is also linked to the sustainable one. You can't solve one problem without confronting another, so replicating what's next door creates a problem that compromises the performance of the project. Another way to think of it is that the problem is the solution. In other words of you have a given problem the constraints of the problem is usually what lead to innovation. The idea is that heritage and history are this problem and then became the solution to our problem. We're saying the same thing about the terraced house next door but we are saying it in a contemporary way, and we're asking questions of what it should be, not necessarily making a statement. A contemporary building can say it in a contemporary voice. Now we can talk about what we're going to do in the future rather than mull over what we did for the last hundred years.

I was able to do these experiments because it was my own project. When you ask somebody else, it's easier because you're external to the process, but when I design a house for myself it's daunting, you discover things about yourself. You get this doubt, you wonder, "Is this who I am, is this what I should be doing?" Then falling without a net can be very confronting, but that brings the best out in this as well.

I've been to many cities around the world, and at the risk of sounding like I have a parochial bias, Melbourne is such a great city. It is not through design, it's by evolution. If you think about the grid, all the laneways we have were originally designed to be egress spaces for services. It was fiercely debated whether they should be there because of crime and disease and so forth, but now not only do people use them, they define Melbourne. This is a good thing because we are becoming an urbanized people. We can't just erase our cities and start over from scratch, that would be a tragedy. What we need to do is adapt our cities. **"**

ARCHITECT
CASEY BROWN ARCHITECTURE
MUNGEE, AUSTRALIA
2007
18 SQUARE METERS

[PERMANENT CAMPING]

Penny Clay

Penny Clay

Think of what would be the perfect apartment building. The complex is close to direct transit to downtown and in a thriving neighborhood. The front units are staggered to provide light for the buildings behind, and the relationship to the street acts as a buffer between the public and private spaces. A sympathetic use of material, massing, and details all are environmentally applied to provide character. Natural light and ventilation are introduced through a gracious placement of windows, shading, and corridors. Ample balconies act as shade for the residences below in summer. Rainwater is captured for the public garden and private courtyard. Solar, thermal mass, ventilation stacks, and glass act in unison to passively provide comfort year around. Then just add thermal hot water and PV onto the roof to maintain self-reliance. Take all of this perfectly climate-suited dense housing and give it to low-income residents.

When visiting the site a resident invited me into her top floor studio. She has lived there since its completion, and her enthusiasm is best expressed by the jungle of plants she maintains on the patio. The space was small but lofty with the angled windows providing a unique perch above the forward courtyard. Her happiness is perhaps the most effective measure of the project's success.

ARCHITECT
DESIGNINC
MELBOURNE, AUSTRALIA
2007
4800 SQUARE METERS

[K2 APARTMENTS]

JOHN MACDONALD

At DesignInc, we look at many building elements as having more than just one benefit. Mies van der Rohe coined the term "less is more," but with all of our buildings, we strive to achieve "more with less." When you look at the multiple benefits of this approach to design it helps control costs and also delivers benefits beyond the scope of the brief.

The design industry has achieved great things globally over the past few years in rating systems such as LEED and the Green Stars program in Australia. This is a testament of our ability to adapt to new challenges and educate our clients on issues of environmental importance. We now need to develop more collaborative ways of working and learning so we can better advocate for broader system change to secure our shared future.

Over the next few years, a number of leaders will emerge who are risk-takers and collaborators, experimenters and innovators. We should not be looking at closed-door design secrets but open-door sharing of ideas between all stakeholders as we act to decarbonize the building sector and lead the way implementing resilient and regenerative self sustaining communities for the future. The whole idea is to move beyond rating systems to make a positive impact.

Amory Lovin's book *Natural Capitalism*, written a number of years ago now, has a seminal diagram showing that adding new technologies and systems increases the construction cost, but when you adopt an integrated design approach, you are able to break through the barrier and begin to save money. That has resonated very well with me. We have tried to do that with a number of our buildings. For instance, in one of our early low energy buildings for

Deakin University in Melbourne, we were able to achieve lower energy consumption and construction costs by using a hollow core slab system, which both acted as the mechanical ductwork and provided thermal mass from exposed concrete ceilings.

In Melbourne, we have a regular climate effect in summer where pressure cells come across our continent every three or four days and create a spike in temperature. So we are able to create a comfort range using the thermal lag effect of the mass of the building to take out those spikes in temperature. Melbourne is fortunate to have a high diurnal temperate range between day and night in summer. We utilized this phenomenon of pressure cells and night cooling in our well-publicized CH2 Melbourne City Council office building which we designed in conjunction with City of Melbourne. CH2 was the first six-star Green Star building designed and built in Australia and is considered a world leader internationally. Using operable windows, the Council is able to flush heat out of the building at night and "recharge" the concrete slab ceilings with cool night air, lower internal temperatures for the next day without mechanical air conditioning. With exposed thermal mass you can provide 15 to 20% free energy, which can allow cooling systems to be downsized. This approach works in Melbourne. It would not be successful in hotter and more humid climates so it is essential to design passive solutions specifically for the local climate and geography.

The K2 Apartments is a sustainable social housing project consisting of 96 units in Melbourne for the Victorian Government Office of Housing. This project is essentially the residential equivalent of the CH2 building in terms of innovation. Our

design was chosen in a competition open to all Victorian architects. In the design, we thought carefully about all the passive design principles, good orientation, sun control, insulation, thermal mass, and cross ventilation. Like CH2, the principles of thermal mass were very important. Due to single loaded access walkways, the building allows for excellent cross ventilation. In Melbourne's summer, there is often a breeze in the afternoon, which comes off Port Phillip Bay nearby. The single loaded corridors allow breezes to pass through the building from one side to the other.

The architectural form evolved from a direct expression of the environmental criteria. Living spaces are all oriented towards the north, making it possible to get winter sun into the living areas for natural solar heating so there is a reduced need for heating in the building. It was also important to get the glazing ratios right, as many buildings have too much glass.

K2 has interesting elevations with a variety of modular planned complexity expressed in the façades. Sun control was also an important design consideration, and the balconies above were used to shade the units below. The top floors, which we called Pods, are self-shading and formed a different type of architecture on top.

We stepped the buildings back from four to eight stories to get the massing right in terms of scale and allow sunlight into internal landscaped courtyards. There are four blocks, which all vary in height to suit sun penetration, and are linked by a green spine, which also collects water and connects to an internal communal courtyard. We added some active systems solar PVs and solar hot water on the roofs but the focus was primarily on good passive design. In the competition brief, the client

briefed a low energy integrated passive solar design and a building that did not look like a common public housing project. From an environmental aspect, the building uses 70% less energy than a typical apartment building, which is quite a radical reduction.

We were also very interested in sustainable materials. For instance, we found some wharf pilings from the docks in Melbourne and used them to form the circulation spine at K2. In the selection of recycled timbers, we were concerned about the chain of custody of the material, from its source to its final use. We developed a comprehensive selection of materials based on low embodied energy, durability, robustness, toxicity, reuse/recyclability, and biodiversity. As a result, K2 is a very durable and low maintenance building. The tenants express a sense of pride living there. It has been well maintained and it's looking almost as good today as when it was built. The building has mellowed with the timbers overtime but that was the intention. There are very few painted finishes so there is very little maintenance from that point of view. Public housing needs to be very robust to withstand the rigors of its occupants and the intercity environment. There is no graffiti at K2, a testament to the pride that good design can instill in residents. The project is also in a great location near the Melbourne CBD and close to public transport, which supports a very low-impact lifestyle for the tenants.

Most people think that the only way to achieve high densities is with high-rise towers but K2 creates quite a high density in a medium rise development with a strong interface and activation with the street. K2 is as much about community integration as it is about sustainability. The social aspect of the communal spaces is based on a central nervous system with a transition from the public to private. The front of the complex has a public courtyard, which is also used for educational purposes with display panels to communicate the principles of the project. It is an ongoing process educating the tenants on how to best use the building. That is a challenge for buildings in general. A building may have good design principles but in operation many fall short of the mark.

Our team is deeply engaged in the emerging sciences, technologies, biomimicry and biophilia in the pursuit of developing positive impact, regenerative cities. Biomimicry and biophilia are interesting as generators of architectural form but in terms of functional materiality, they are fascinating as well. Nature does everything very efficiently and it also produces everything locally, it doesn't require containers from Italy to survive. Doing everything locally is something certainly to learn from nature.

I think that in the future we might have biologists in our design team. The research that nature has been conducting for

thousands or millions of years inspires us. We are doing studies of regenerative buildings, which are the aspirational "holy grail," and are now technically possible. We have the technological skill in biological systems to design regenerative buildings and cities now. The potential is that buildings can improve the environment: they generate clean power, purify the air, and process waste and water. On a precinct basis, this approach works even better.

When we work together in multi-disciplinary teams using integrated design, we can make quantum leaps rather than incremental change improvements. Collaboration is key to this. We invest our time at universities helping in education and in public advocacy. We see this as an important part of what we do. I believe this is the way we are going to make substantial progress. It is not just working with consultants and larger teams but with other architects and sharing ideas.

I believe the Australian approach to architecture provides freshness to our design that is expressed in the form and high level of innovation in our buildings. Perhaps it is due to a touch of the Aussie larrikin. We have a cultural resourcefulness and willingness to take risks in our work. Getting "more for less" from our efforts is seen as a common sense approach to producing a beautiful, regenerative legacy for future generations. **"**

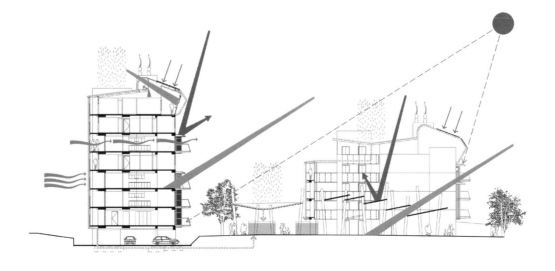

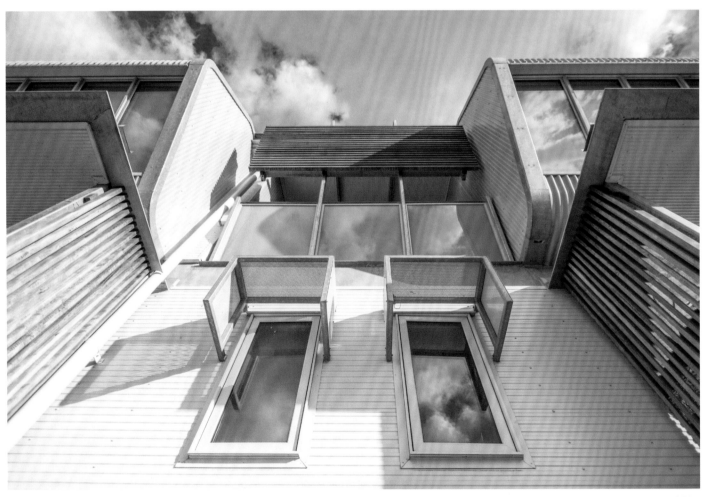

Australians are by definition sports crazy, so naturally sports architecture should play a significant role in the nation's psyche. Sport clubs dot the suburbs like fire stations, but none has the kinetic punch and environmental acumen as Templestowe Reserve Sporting Pavilion. The new sport center packs a lot of solar technology on the roof to support the many hot showers taken inside. It also uses the thermal mass from the deconstruction of the previous building buried below, which acts as a heat sink for incoming fresh air to help cool down exerted bodies.

The charged design is the real story because it acts as an active participant in the games. Every viewing angle gives a new formulation of massing and gesture to keep you on your toes. Just approaching the entrance takes a little bravery because the building reaches out to grasp you. Inspired by the bolts on team uniforms, the saw tooth roof points skywards, concealing the solar electric and thermal panels. But with all the angular bravado, the jutting brickwork, zigzag rails leading to the turf, makes an adventure of traversing the pavilion.

[TEMPLESTOWE RESERVE SPORTING PAVILION]

ARCHITECT
PHOOEY ARCHITECTS
TEMPLESTOWE, MELBOURNE, AUSTRALIA
2009

PETER HO

We're very fortunate in Melbourne that we have a culturally diverse society. They're prepared to challenge and discuss the perception of what they like or don't like. It's not a bad thing, it adds to the abundance and diversity of our society that consequently makes a much richer environment around us. That's why it's important to look at something like Templestowe Reserve Sporting Pavilion in terms of designing a building. Yes it's a climate-neutral building, that's great, but the thing that's most important about it is how you engage in the design process with the whole community. The sporting reserve is for cricket as well as football for junior level, little tackers, as well as older players in high level of competition.

Templestowe is an established suburban neighborhood 40 minutes from the city core, the fact that it's one of our oldest suburbs makes it a very strong community. What I think is interesting, if we just look at the sports themselves, is that kids who grow up here all aspire to be great footballers and great cricketers. That's what we have here in Melbourne. We play on the local grounds inspired by this greatness, and the interesting thing about these clubs in terms of how to actually survive is that their identity continues to change because different organizations have to support them. So, while they may start off with a black jumper, it may turn into a jumper that is supported by somebody from interstate, so it will have a different rip through the jumper or pattern. So the name might stay the same but the colors change. It's much more dynamic than compared to what we see in the high levels where that identity is much stronger. How do you capture that identity and history of the club that constantly changes?

The Templestowe Reserve Sporting Pavilion's form is trying to capture all of those qualities as jumpers have changed and how those forms are represented

in the building. The locals jokingly call it the Sydney Opera House of sporting pavilions. It has an identity, people know where they're going, and it has some of the qualities of a jumper on the front of the building. We have the whole front facade doing a Mexican wave to generate activity around the football match. How do you start one and how do you continue it especially at a local football ground when there are only 10 or 20 people around the boundary line? Somebody's got to start it, which is always the hardest part. So there's a bit of whimsy in the approach, a bit of entertainment and a laugh out of it as well. There are qualities that are expressed as a consequence of that building.

The roof is a vernacular to the neighborhood but is also functional by supporting the photovoltaics and thermal panels that are on the roof. We appreciate that if we are actually trying to create a climate-neutral building and a sporting Pavilion, that the thing we consume the most is in fact hot water in that space. We have daylighting in many of the areas.

Different parts of the building reference different qualities and outcomes for how it is used. For instance, the run-thoroughs or entrances to change rooms and the brickwork pattern were intended to be a lot more broken, like a wall tumbling down. So the building itself needs to be a spectator for the little kids running through.

All the buildings that were previous we had to demolish so we cut a giant hole underneath the building with the building itself sitting off the ground, and all of that thermal mass was made use of. We pass air over it to cool before it goes into the community space. We are able to do all kinds of different tricks and also think about how all those materials might work from an upcycle perspective. How the materials have more value than new stone potentially. I am interested in the building processes of how we understand the relationship

of the material at an urban level. This is what my PhD is in. What I am doing right now is extremely influenced by the way that William McDonough thinks, and my specific interests are how to make that an architectural quality. We see ourselves a bit like MacGyver with his paper clip on-site and wondering what to do next, how to solve the next problem. So what are the things that we have learned to be able to do that?

For the project I'm working on right now as I go around to all these manufacturers and visit the people who make glass, I see all the waste that comes from their process. It's the most energy-intensive process, the tax they pay for all the energy is completely ridiculous, the waste the comes from the manufacturer of the glass, people who can recycle parts of the waste part already completely overloaded in terms of their capacity to deal with it. So, to actually work out how to reuse that as a material, in a very interesting possible way, is the challenge. The potential expression of that is very exciting. The question is in the way that we design and the economic benefit to everyone involved in the process. This is what I'm learning from the guys who produce the stuff. It's one thing to create a potential opportunity for something but it's got to be done in a way that's actually going to save money. If I think about that in my design perspective from what we're doing in the office, it's great that we can tackle that problem from a design perspective and do it in our own ways.

The Carpet Couch 2 in the entry of this building came from the carpet we pulled out from our office up here. We all have the need to make an appealing place, but most people are willing to change fabrics and just throw them out, but that's just something that we think we can turn into something much richer, to think that the carpet on the floor is now a couch and has a complete next life that provides comfort.

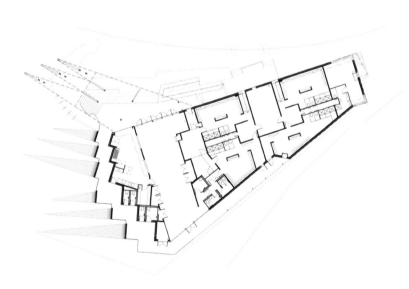

ARCHITECT
STUDIO505
MELBOURNE, AUSTRALIA
2010
1136 SQUARE METERS
6 STARS GREENSTAR, LEED PLATINUM

[PIXEL BUILDING]

If you know anything about sustainable design then chances are you have come across the Pixel Building. It is a building you cannot unsee, which is studio 505's design mission. The project has racked up more LEED and Green Star points than any other project in history, has more mentions in the building media, and has a reputation of being the bad boy in the amicable green culture.

The four-story project is surprisingly diminutive in person considering its public reputation. Once you get past the kinetic visual bravado, it is a very gentle systems approach to energy, materials, and water. The project is a rational machine designed to squeeze out every drop of water and energy onsite.

Let's say you're a raindrop. You may get very lucky and fall onto the vegetated roof and get pumped into the rainwater-storage tank. You will be filtered and then used to wash a human hand. Now you will find yourself in the exterior planter bed being filtered again and reused in the shower. Your third trip around you may be used to flush the toilet, and while you will now head to the street sewer system you helped the anaerobic digester create methane to heat water for the raindrops that follow after you.

The project's concrete is specially formulated to reduce the carbon footprint by 50% with an unprecedented 92% gross weight of recycled and reclaimed content. The renewable energy systems are more traditional with mixed results when it comes to the Vertical Axis Wind Turbines. What is decided is that the project is an aggressively successful experiment in systems integration. This level of organized thinking is what has made the Pixel Building a conversation piece long after you decide if you like how it looks.

DB: We looked long and hard at the facade which needed to be a sign, a symbol of what we're doing. If you built a boring building out there which was super sustainable and all that sort of stuff people would drive past and not even see it. You lose an edge to your message. At the same time, what was important to us was not to use sustainability as a "style," timber slats, nuts and berries, recycle this and that, you can tell the building looked sustainable. But it was important for us that it did not become a situation where to have a sustainable building you have to choose a particular style. We want to show that you could create a sustainable building that did not look like a sustainable building, but it does not look like any other building either. It does not have to be a double skinned German style high-tech, or conversely nuts and berries.

You look at CH2, which has got plastic bags and widgets, wood panels, and all those sort of things, every facade is different because it has a different agenda in terms of solar access. Passive House is a very interesting set of rules, we looked at it for Delta, and although we did not look at it for Pixel it has been designed in almost the exact same way as a super heavily insulated box. There is one piece of single-pane glass, which is rounded and we fought tooth and nail to keep because they wanted single pane faceted glass. The building was run through the Australian Green building Councils 6 star–rating program for version four of the offices.

We knew our strategy was successful when our marketing manager found an article out of the Financial Review and it had a big picture on it of Pixel. Not once in the article was the building referred to but the article is about sustainability embedded in the

banking sector or something like that. They put the picture there because everyone said oh yeah "sustainability." We kind of branded the idea of excessive performance. We didn't have to choose those colors or to choose those shapes, it would've performed exactly the same with dark gray rectangles that striped the building and looked like a louver. But it does change the interior radically when every floor has a different color you're looking through.

We have a green swell on the outside the building, which takes the graywater and filters it. Unfortunately, it's not working at all right now because there is nobody in the building; the rainwater tank is overflowing into the graywater supply, which feeds the green swell, which runs around the edge.

DZ: The objective of the water system was twofold, using rainwater and graywater. We wanted to look at the whole water cycle, which is something we really want to make a feature of this building because at that time we were in a massive drought. Sustainable architecture in Australia tends to look up at the sun all the time, and we felt that water at that point in time was a much bigger concern to implement because we were running out of it. New rules came out such as you cannot use potable water on your garden, for instance, so with these new restrictions we wanted to see what's possible. How little water could we use?

DB: We take the rainwater and put it in a tank, we treated it and for its first round of use into the showers and toilets and sinks. The blackwater goes from the vacuum toilet to the anaerobic digester which we use for the methane gas fired hot water unit. The graywater itself is filtered from showers and basins, except for the kitchen sink, which goes to the blackwater. Graywater is screened and filtered before it is directed

into this living edge. This is basically a planter box wrapped around the exterior of the building. The roof is designed as a xeriscape using native Victorian grasses, allowing rainwater to collect for the building's use. You know you're learning when one side of the roof is thriving and another side is dying. We want to see both be nearly dead so we can gauge the threshold of success or failure, that's why there are three beds on the roof.

On top there are three tracking solar panels so there is a symbiosis between them and the plants, we get an amplification of rain in some places and others you get a shadow. A weather station measures sunlight, wind, relative humidity, and temperature. So basically the building is able to record a series of parallel outputs from the solar trackers. For instance, some people say that solar trackers are 40% more effective than fixed solar, but are they really? I don't know, so we document it. The tracking units each cost $4,500. So is it really more efficient, how long do we need to offset its cost? You know there's all these things we talk about like double skinned walls that ventilate, that's great but we have to test to see if it's worth it.

DZ: As far as the planters, there are quite a few buildings past 20 years that have integrated planters and they all worked without the water restrictions that came into place. Suddenly you could only use collected water from on-site, so they had to be switched off. The plants of course died, and people got very upset about it, so the trend was against integrated planters. What we are doing here is capturing our own water to water our own planters, but we never thought the building would never be occupied. There is also an architectural element of comfort where people sitting on the inside have this very expressive shading that is this little garden which is in situ, between the facade and the shading.

DB: So, that is an improvement on the indoor quality due to the garden out there. It also provides a shading ledge; it is in a place the Council allowed us to build based on an archaic rule to allow fancy pediments on top of buildings. And what we did was create 140 linear meters graywater green swell, a nice garden bed to look at, shading shelf to improve the performance of the facade, and you can maintain and clean windows by using that as a walk.

Given enough water in the facade's green swell that comes all the way through, it is good enough to go back into the rainwater tank. The snake has bit its own tail, close the loop so the only extra water you need is coming from the rain, the only extra you're taking away remains in people's bodies, evaporates, or goes through the black water system. Every time we turn the tap on it takes tremendous resources to provide us with what we consider "fresh." There is no "fresh water," every drop of this planet has been dinosaur piss, in bodies and so forth, it's just that we have an excellent filtration system here on Earth, I love it.

I love Jason McLennan and the Living Building Challenge premise that all the current rating tools are about how less bad that you can make your building and he is saying you're operating on the wrong side of positive—we are still saying "we only use" or "20% less."

But we find the biggest challenge is if the clients are willing to go to that place. We use our enthusiasm as best we can to say, "Are you prepared to pay us to think about and deliver to you this outcome?" A building like Pixel is really great for us. While the building scored all the points in the green star system we walk in and say we

can do that better or we can use a different material, but the idea of its operation is there. The client Grocon wanted to take this technology, which is brand new, and make it woven together into this building. The net result is we've been able to take things out of the building like the ductwork.

DZ: When you go to the site it looks deceivingly simple because the real achievements in the building are all the things we took away. The floor plate is incredibly empty, the ceiling is just this concrete thing with suspended lights, and you wonder where is all the other stuff. We have trickle ventilation in the floor but there's only one return element.

DB: Vacuum toilets are one the most brilliant technologies for tall towers because at the moment tall towers are designed around transferring toilets from out of the core to the core, and around lifts and all that. But if you have a vacuum toilet in a raised floor they don't need to be in the core, they can be anywhere you want and naturally ventilated. You basically drive all of that from a fan through a 50-millimeter pipe.

DZ: We found out that hydronic services and towers are the most out of date technology in large buildings. In the most high-tech buildings, everything is still just gravity fed. Using a vacuum toilet and anaerobic digester we massively reduce the water we need. Now we can run our services in a built-up floor which helps you with your acoustics, yet creates much more freedom for your bathroom. Your vertical drains can be smaller and wherever you want. There are a lot of things we learned from doing Pixel that we are applying.

When you look at the roof, the photovoltaics are not really designed around aesthetics, they are sitting there like a monitoring station. People criticize that

part of the building for its aesthetics, but it was conceived as a laboratory and side office. That's what took so long to integrate and balance all these systems.

The facade's geometry came from 2,400 x 1,200 standard building sheets of modules. By cutting the sheets down into shapes we do not waste material and the panels are not at all reminiscent of the sheets. We vetted all the panels on the facade to make sure we use all the panels on-site. We went through quite a few iterations where our initial vision was that the building could close, like peacock feathers. Because of budget we could not make it movable so we had to come up with a static facade that still expressed the vividness of our original vision of opening up. We needed to achieve 100% daylight penetration to the floor so from inside the building looking at certain directions the shading disappears. For the outside we chose colors to make into swirls you can read from the corner. The colors are selected to stand out- greys, oranges, and whites.

We wanted to use concrete because Grocon was very well known for concrete construction and is still Australia's most advanced concrete contractor. They developed together with RMIT a special concrete that uses the highest concentration recycled content in the mix, upwards of 90%, and displaces half the cement. They want to demonstrate they could build commercial high-strength concrete. They call it Pixelcrete and have actually won an award for its development.

DB: There is a great cartoon from a cartoonist in Australia who did this picture of a guy sitting in a house on a really hot day with a fan on the table blowing onto his face, and the cable goes out and connects to a wind turbine. You think, just get out of the f##king house. And it's the same with running lights from the solar panel. ""

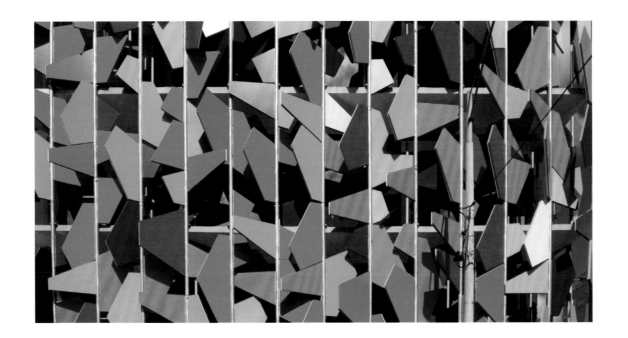

studio 505

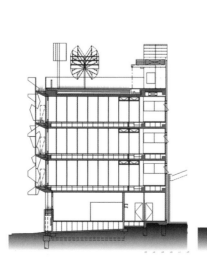

Melbourne's downtown grid ends at the newly developed Docklands, a brownfield site quickly being filled with an eclectic array of corporate headquarters and apartments by the Yarra River, just before it makes its final turn into Port Phillip Bay. Next to the river's edge is the ANZ Centre, a sprawling groundscraper, which is a new connection between the river and the city.

The open design of the bank's headquarters serves as an antidote to the many towers of Melbourne that sit nameless above the lively streets below. The interior merges corporate life with the public in a great experiment of open design. The perforated ground floor and two large atriums connect to the next 12 levels, making it the largest open office in the world. The street's historic bluestone sidewalks carry through into the building making the ground floor a pedestrian street, servicing the 7,000 plus employees and visitors, and amending the lack of services in the nascent neighborhood.

While the experience of entering can be overwhelming at first, playful insertions enlivens the massive open floor plan, with the first four levels based a central theme. The eclectically designed interior, set from somber natural tones to primary colors and oversized objects, brings the expanse down to a manageable scale and severs the siloed behavior of the employees.

While the bank's program is to introduce human scale to a corporate identity, the environmental impact of the project is equally as detailed. Photovoltaic panels and vertical axes wind generators dot the roof, a tri-generation power plant reduces the facilities CO_2 by 70%, and river water cooling is used for the air conditioning. To this, include an extensive black and grey water reclamation system as well as rainwater collection, and the building is very much an environmental village cloaked as an office building.

ARCHITECT
HASSELL STUDIOS
DOCKLANDS, MELBOURNE, AUSTRALIA
2010
130,000 SQUARE METERS
6 STARS GREENSTAR

[ANZ CENTRE]

ROB BACKHOUSE

One of the things we often talk about is that issue of how you can make such large buildings in the city live and breathe, be much more permeable. The new Docklands neighborhood is a bit awkward because most of the ground plans are elevated because you can't excavate the land there. The idea is to have a piazza in the middle of the building, anyone can wander in and see and hopefully engage with the bank. Permeability was a big issue for us and the bank, for what they wanted to achieve in such a big building. We explained to ANZ what we were going to give them—whether they knew what they were getting is maybe another thing. One of the things ANZ was trying to do, and I think all the banks, is to seem more transparent and hopefully even more approachable to their customers and to the shareholders and the communities where they exist. A lot of it can be seen as some kind of sinister PR campaign, a lot of Australia's wealth is probably tied up in the banking system. So, being accessible to the public and their shareholders is pretty important, I think. That building being so big, consolidating so many parts of their business into one headquarters, not being a fortress was really important.

Imagine 7,000 desks, which can hold up to 8,000 people. The building is 130,000 square meters gross including the car park, retail, and office space, I think it's the largest building in the southern hemisphere. It's more approachable rather than being a ridiculous tower and not getting the sense of what's inside. You can wander into the bottom of this building as a member of the public. You can have a coffee there, generally walk through and access the riverfront from Collins Street. Melbourne

has never really had that sort of amenity to get from its main business address straight to the river. Allowing the public and community access was a pretty big step for ANZ.

The other force that was at play was the authorities saying that because it is such a big building and, that because of the original master plan of Docklands, it had to be transversal. We had to take out a street to build over two blocks. We were able to convince ANZ that this was aligned with their vision and their aspiration, which is to be accessible, approachable, and transparent. In the end, it was a happy collision. We had a lot of security people say, "You can't do it, it won't work, you have to lock it down, you can't let the public here."

They were used to being in more conventional towers with small floor plates, and one business unit wouldn't talk to another. They wouldn't share a meeting room let alone a cookie, they were that siloed. For the bank's organizational structure to completely explode all those conventional silos and structures that constrained people was a pretty massive shift. When we did a lot of briefing with them they talked about openness and transparency, connectivity and all those aspirations to have people more integrated. Those are just words, right? I remember going to a big bank in London on Canary Wharf to do research on where we're going to go with this. It was a big tower, and I noticed a couple of pocket atriums that connected a few floors. I remember saying, "Ahhh, this is what not to do." They have gone from one generation of workspace to another but none of the descriptions were

really there. They tried to get there but didn't make it.

When it comes to sustainability the bank increased the budget significantly. There are a few approaches to how they targeted sustainability. One was the systems and technology in the building. They spent an extra $35 million on a $470 million budget on the building to get from what we call five-star to a six-star rating. Because they are the owner-occupier, they saw the payback as being a no-brainer. They saw this building on their balance sheet for 20 to 30 years; they are not going to be here for the short-term. Some of the technologies may be a bit more symbolic. People argue about will the wind turbines really contribute to the energy balance of the building. Some of the things were ANZ saying we want people to know that we're willing to invest in things coming, even if it's not a huge ticket item: the river water–cooling and tri-generation, and I think one of the largest rooftop solar electric arrays, the green rooftops, and the water catchment. The water catchment system reduces the potable water consumption by 60 to 70% of normal office building. The carbon output is also 60 to 70% less than a normal building. I think water and carbon are two particularly big issues in Australia. While these were not big-ticket items, ANZ was willing to invest in what they say they want to do. Something that really reduces energy and is very uncommon here was the under floor air conditioning system. So this was a big step for services and technology for a building of this scale in Australia, outside of the Council House by DesignInc and the Bond Building by Lend Lease. Nothing in the corporate sector had gone that far really investing in it being six-star and being defined as a world leader in sustainable design. The other architectural elements like the shading and facade types, maybe are not as beautiful as the Bligh Tower in Sydney, but it all worked.

The plan's form is very much related to how it relates to the sinuous nature of the river. We wanted to create an architectural form that was not fighting with the context. There was a concern because it's a big lump of a building, so you have to break down that sense of it being a monolith, which I think it does to some degree. The other aspect is the way they are using the building now in terms of sustainability. It was designed to be used as what we call a flexible working model. Not everyone has their own desk; there were multiple places in there so people can come and go from the other ANZ buildings. They can use the building in a much more agile way. So originally, they moved in with 6,500 desks for 6,500 people. In a study of how many actual people were in the building at any one time, it was never more than 4,500 people. People are meeting with clients or doing other aspects of the business. Working out how to use it better as an energy proposition, let alone what they invested in was one of their motivations. They have this great building,

it has all the settings in it, technology and diversity, many ways to do things, so pushing its utilization higher is a major goal. I think that's true for the whole of Australia, the buildings are being utilized much more intensely. This is probably one of the biggest examples of where they're trying to use the flexible workspace into a building of that scale.

It's a little city within the city. There are the systems and the architecture, then how the building is used is about sustainability as well. Melbournites, I think, are really critical of Docklands, and maybe I am a little self-conscious. Docklands does not have the fine grain in it as Melbourne as a city has. But what attracted the big corporations was that very close to the city they could have a big urban campus where they can consolidate their businesses. They had an opportunity to create these groundscrapers, to get out of the skyscrapers. The downside of that is that we don't have the laneways, the little buildings and the things that made downtown Melbourne so successful. I don't know how successful it will be, when you look at the fact that Docklands is only half finished. So when it is 100% finished, those niches and pop-ups and edges start to occur and I kind of think they will. For our project we try to suck that into the building, and I

think when you get in there it does buzz. In fact, Melbourne 10 years ago is nothing like it is now, there is a lot of stuff happening downtown now.

One other dimension of ANZ that is loosely under the sustainability hat is diversity in terms of population. The bank saw the critical need to accommodate diversity, so now as they have become what they call a super regional bank where they have business in China, parts of India, and Southeast Asia. They see their workforce is not only more multicultural but multigenerational. If you look at the interior, it is not just one thing over and over again. There is a lot of diversity designed into the space. There's character and functionality that hopefully serves that diverse population. We've also brought the bluestone from Melbourne's sidewalks into the interior, and the timber was for the sense of warmth. We wanted a softer, more approachable palette because of the scale of the building. Even if you look at just the paving on the main floor, it was about how do you create a much finer grain? There different scales to the pavers that run across the entire level as opposed to making a corporate foyer that is just a repeating slab of granite. 🙶

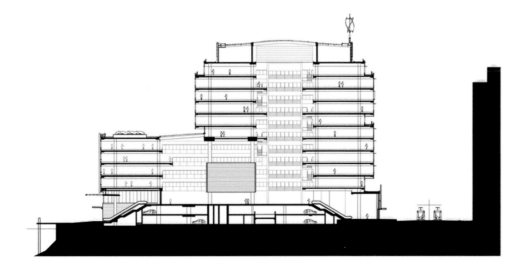

ARCHITECT
DURBACH BLOCK JAGGERS
CANBERRA, AUSTRALIA
2002
5000 SQUARE METERS

[COMMONWEALTH PLACE]

Commonwealth Place is a contemporary insertion into the radial masterplan of Walter Burley Griffin and Marion Mahony Griffin's Canberra. The Australian national capital is the continent's largest inland city, located as a compromise between Melbourne and Sydney. The century-old centrally planned vision of urban idealism, much like the modernist based Brasilia, lacks ground level vitality. The site is at the tip of the inner city radial spoke from the Parliament House to Burley Griffin Lake. Envisioned as a town square in the design competition brief, Durbach Block Jaggers instead inserted a folded lawn, introducing the desire of play in the form of a green crown.

The project is an interpretation of the rolling hills of the area. It is first cleaved, flipped, and then pushed to the sides to make way for the grand access through the capital. Tucked under the sides are a restaurant and gallery, opening the program up to the sidewalk. Despite the grandiose plans of a nation's seat of power, it is now a place for children to roll down a grassy hill, or bike through a man made chasm.

I was fortunate to visit on a pristine April afternoon, which was also Anzac Day, a remembrance of the first Australian foreign battle. Commonwealth Place seemed to be the city's cradle of activity. Bikers flowed through the incision, a path to the old capital. Rollerbladers, Segways, and skateboarders followed suit. A father and sons played ball against the sandstone wall while others sat on either side of the inclined lawn to take it all in. After a decade of use the place was just getting broken in.

ND: A lot of what we do is because it is amusing in a way. You don't tell clients that, but you know you're just having a good time. It's hard work but essentially what you're doing is incredibly pleasurable, it's not exactly saving lives. I do think Australia's very open about this, especially Melbourne. Sydney is a little bit tighter. In Melbourne, there's a sense of, "what about this, or what about that!"

Architecture in Australia is history-free in a funny way. And this new architecture is not just for adapting to climates because in Melbourne, where the shift is happening most profoundly, they have the mildest climate.

I think Peter Corrigan and Robin Boyd were super important cracking that open, like how Robert Venturi was important for American architecture. Whereas our building in Canberra is trying to be serious about the context, it has also inverted some of the conditions that were inherent in the competition. They wanted a traditional square with shops around it. We asked what if you inverted the two end conditions, which are the two mountains, and turn it into a gathering place, quite literally like an open hand. The axis now passes through those two mountains.

CB: The expectation in Canberra, because it is not a very urban place, is to see the grid as a kind of a sacred axis set up by Walter Griffin from one hill to the next. If you are in the Commonwealth Place in winter, when it is often empty, it feels like a piece of the lawn is folded. It wouldn't feel like an empty town square, you know, the tumbleweed blowing through the space that nobody ever goes to. There are so many large spaces that are hard paved and unsustainable,

so changing it to a lawn is very much a materials choice. We're asking what it feels like to be a on a lawn, to not interrupt the flow of that big land axis and if it's full or empty doesn't matter.

ND: We replaced an urban square with a garden and I think that is what attracted the jury. The space is very abstract and I think some people are very annoyed by that abstraction rather than the symbolic potential of a town square which is what I think they're looking for. This is a very sentimental part of Australia. That was the early criticism of the design, that it had no overt symbolic sensibilities. And there are a lot of things that came in afterwards that we had no control over, like the dock.

CB: It's quite hard to say where our project begins and ends because there is a second competition for the space where the path was to run. The winning project was this big mound, so now the ramp, which should have gone straight through, winds around this. One of the problems with Canberra is that you never quite know where you are going, you can't quite see it because everything is so spaced and the roads are so bent. So the idea is that you can look up and say, "oh, that's the old Parliament House," with the idea that you can make these links between these monuments. That experience is frustrated by the final layout, which was determined after the construction began of our project.

NB: Before, the ground kind of slowly tapered, it wasn't a big gesture, more gentle like an airplane taking off. We did make a lot of enemies trying to have them change the design but they did not change anything. So, it was a good introduction to politics for us.

CB: It's funny because you can't really control the edges of your project. But, when it's conceived in one way and ends up slightly distorted, you always wonder if it would have been better the other way. Unlike a house where you can say were one project ends as another begins, some people often confuse our project with the other adjacent one.

It is interesting that the space does not really have a direction. We have seen pictures of kites flying where the whole space comes alive from the sky, then they project movies onto the stonewall, and bands play on the paved walkway where you can see them from either side. It's a simple form that has many orientations, ways of being used as a gathering space. I think it's quite forgiving for an urban space, not as prescriptive. It's also nice to see a space that's used in a way that you could not have anticipated, it becomes completely altered by the way it is used. There were two commercial spaces left empty when we designed it, and they put in an art gallery on one side and a restaurant on the other.

We said we wanted to tile this building like Gaudí, there was a kind of forgiveness in that, like if you say it has a green roof people think, "All right, at least your heart's in place." This project was at the point of the early days of green roofs. There are some issues about how the roof will be held at an angle. Mowing it was a big issue—there is concern about how steep an angle could you mow it. There were a few contentious conversations about that and you never know what in the project is going to bite you in the bum. That's like any project, we can design everything until you get the maintenance crew and they say, "No!" Then you think to yourself, all right, we will have to come up with something else.

ND: When a project is finished it is finished. It's almost not yours anymore so you go back and you think, "that's quite an interesting project."

CB: It was quite fun when we were at an awards night and we were marching through the space with a whole group of architects. It was evening and we hadn't seen the project for years, and although Neil and I did not drink much, everyone else was. We talked and chatted and walked along the flagpoles and then turned left into the space. And there is this one very drunk architect who is standing there going, "Wa, this is fantastic!" And he was shouting to hear the echo. It is actually a lovely moment because it was totally unscripted and he genuinely enjoyed it.

ND: The ramp is also very popular for skateboards and along the walls we commissioned an artwork. We got these aerial photographs of Australia from miles above and chopped them up and put them in strips of glass. The technology was very new at the time and so the photos began to fade immediately, so the Australian landscape is slowly vanishing. It was quite huge: there were these amazing images of the beach and the desert, all in strips.

CB: The flags were a given condition. You want to do something that is quite respectful of them. People worry about flags because there's a lot of invested meaning in them. We wanted to do something that was gentle enough to sit in between them and not be too bombastic. There's a lot of bombastic stuff in Canberra, there's so much civic pretension.

NB: I do have to say architecture is not celebrated that much in Australia.

CB: There is a kind of suspicion about the aspirations of architecture. I think people think that architects are out just to spend their money on a monument to themselves. They are bit suspicious about architects' intentions.

ND: In the end, architecture is all about synthesis. We just synthesize things. I think it is one of the things that is the most precedent-based of all the arts, maybe music as well. You just build on what others have done, there's really very little invention I suspect. Glenn Murcutt is one of the few people who actually invented a language, and it doesn't happen often. You can take anything from Le Corbusier, the smallest detail and it can become a building. That's incredible, he is this endless mind of possibilities and still is today for all of us, I think. Frank Gehry, as good as he is, is this kind of closed system.

CB: Gehry is the language of a trapeze artist while Murcutt is like a pattern book. There's an expectation, and people write briefs like this, that architecture should be like the Bilbao Effect. Give us an icon, give us something memorable. And because of the way buildings are chosen in an architecture competition you have a split-second on a piece of paper to show what the idea is. So everything is nutshelled into these very simplistic one-liner interventions, and buildings are more complex than that. But the vehicle for getting buildings approved and projects through is not.

ND: The subtleties of a building by Luis Kahn would not stand up to competition; they would not even be looked at.

CB: It is kind of like advertising mentality, like a one-liner. 🠒

Jon Gollings

Designing for place means to embrace the people who use it. Architects are assigned a scope for design but that does not mean our designed world should fit into the narrow needs of a few, or even just a majority.

By embracing the needs of homelessness, for instance, the Park Bench House challenges the way society takes care of its own. William McDonough advocates for designers to work for the benefit of all living things, for all time. The Park Bench House responds by saying let's start to design for all people, right now. While never realized beyond a prototype, the project frames the question of design astutely. What is your intention?

ARCHITECT
SEAN GODSELL ARCHITECTS
ANYWHERE
2002

[PARK BENCH HOUSE]

SEAN GODSELL

" I wrote an essay for *Entire Magazine* a couple years ago called, "Any Port in a Storm," that was basically an argument for the Park Bench House. In 2006, we had the Commonwealth games in Melbourne where Commonwealth nations come together in between the Olympics. The city of Melbourne had all the homeless people removed so that visitors could not see them. My question was where did you move them? And then once the games were over do they say you can come back now? It was astonishing that they wanted to pretend that we did not have any homeless people, unlike any other city in the world.

The idea of Park Bench House came out of time I spent in London where I lived in Notting Hill. There was a homeless refuge that was full. You couldn't get a bed so homeless people used to try to get into the Underground station at Notting Hill Gate. So, you'd be running off to work and you have to pick your way around homeless people. London is a pretty harsh place to be homeless because it gets pretty cold.

It's really a comment on the design of urban infrastructure. It's an observation that it doesn't really matter where you are in the world, a subway in New York or Metro in Paris, Underground in London or a park, you go and sit on a bench which usually has metal studs at a certain spacing so you cannot lie down. There's the molded plastic seats with an armrest we see everywhere around the world, which are designed so homeless or vagrant people cannot sleep on them. They're conscious design decisions made across the globe where people are

paid to make those decisions, they are commissioned to do them, and part of the brief is to make sure the people cannot use these.

So it's a commentary on urban infrastructure and a statement that if you shift the paradigm even slightly, you can engage with rather than deny the transient population. We know that they are there but we don't want to see them. This group of people does not have any voice at all, they have no representation. They rely entirely on the goodwill of organizations and charities as well as quirks of design in the city. So the incidental encounter with a doorway or a picnic table or a bench is for want of anything else because there is nothing else.

The idea of the Park Bench House is that you need to change the design only slightly for it to become a rudimentary shelter. Something that can be something else, going back to that magic of childhood saying that isn't what I thought it was. The proposal was that it was a bench during the day, one just flips the lid and it is now a bed. It provides some shelter from the weather, not complete but some. There was a little night light underneath so when the lid came up the light went, you can park your possessions there and try to get a good night sleep. If you can imagine being homeless and how horrible it must be then sleep deprivation is just a given. When you talk to homeless people they always talk about sleeping safely. Homeless people are literally terrified of getting their heads kicked in at night. I want us to see that

potential role for architects in the design of that infrastructure and also a plea to society in general to be slightly more tolerable of those who find themselves in that situation.

We put the Park Bench House into the Institute of Architects awards program for new houses, and we were politely told to get lost by the jury. The reason we put it in there was that here is something that requires them to define, back to me as an architect, what a house is. I can tell you that what we do for less than 1% of the population as a profession is high budget housing for people who can afford to pay for architects is not what most people think a house is.

For some people, a house is a doorway or a bench. So, that was the proposition. Okay yes we have rich people doing beautiful houses, but here are people with no voice or money and they need a house as well. How do you define shelter? When you put all those projects together it's not just a challenge to architects, but also a challenge to people who commission architecture to say why are we always lumped in the exclusive category. We are always talking to the people with lots of money, which is centered on this tiny marketplace for us. So why are we not talking over here all the time as well, where it doesn't have to be commissioned for you to benefit from it. You didn't commission the design of a comfortable chair but you are benefiting from the work. Why not just extend that into the population in need? "

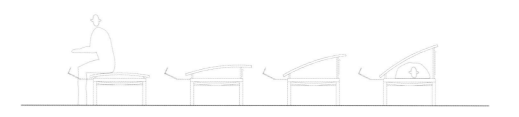

APPENDIX

ARCHITECT LABEL XAIN www.xain.jp,
Sampei, Jun.ichi, Interview 05/06/2013, Tokyo, Japan

ANDREW MAYNARD ARCHITECTS www.maynardarchitects.com
Andrew Maynard and Mark Austin, Interview 03/24/2013, Melbourne, Australia

ALTIER TEKUTO www.tekuto.com
Yasuhiro Yamashita, Interview 03/19/2014, email

BARRIO I PERAIRE ARQUITECTES www.barrioperaire.blogspot.com
Berta Barrio, Interview 10/23/2013, Teià, Spain

BJARKE INGELS GROUP www.big.dk
video by Dr. Trine Jeppesen 9/15/2013

CANVAS ARQUITECTOS www.canvasarquitectos.com
Juan Vicente, Interview 10/30/2013, Salamanca, Spain

CASEY BROWN ARCHITECTURE www.caseybrown.com.au

COLL-BARREU ARQUITECTOS www.coll-barreu-arquitectos.com
Juan Coll-Barreu and Daniel Gutiérrez Zarza, Interview 10/24/2013, Vitoria-Gasteiz, Spain
Juan Coll-Barreu, Interview 10/25/2013, Bilbao, Spain

DESIGNINC www.designinc.com.au
John Macdonald, Interview 08/12/2014, phone

DR. WOLFGANG FEIST www.passiv.de
Interview 09/23/2014, Portland, Maine

DURBACH BLOCK JAGGERS www.durbachblockjaggers.com
Neil Durbach and Camellia Block, Interview 04/26/2013, Sydney, Australia

EDWARD MAZRIA www.architecture2030.org, www.2030palette.org
Interview 02/14/2013, Santa Fe, New Mexico
Originally published on Inhabitat
www.inhabitat.com/interview-ed-mazria-founder-of-architecture-2030-introduces-the-2030-palette

FRANCIS-JONES MOREHEN THORP www.fjmt.com.au

HASSELL STUDIOS www.hassellstudio.com
Rob Backhouse, Interview 04/22/2013, Melbourne, Australia

KAVELLARIS URBAN DESIGN www.kud.com.au
Billy Kavellaris, Interview 04/19/2013, Melbourne, Australia

KMD ARCHITECTS www.kmdarchitects.com
Roberto Velasco, Interview 01/19/2015, phone

KUBOTA ARCHITECTS www.katsufumikubota.jp

LEDERER + RAGNARSDOTTIR + OEI www.archlro.de
Arno Lederer, Interview 12/11/2013, phone

MCDONOUGH + PARTNERS www.mcdonough.com
William McDonough, Interview 08/20/2013, phone

MILLER HULL PARTNERSHIP www.millerhull.com
Brian Court, Interview 02/26/2013, Seattle, Washington

MHN DESIGN UNION www.mhndu.com
Kevin Ng, Interview 04/26/2013, Sydney, Australia

PERKINS+WILL www.perkinswill.com
Peter Busby, Interview 3/27/2013, phone

PHOOEY ARCHITECTS www.phooey.com.au
Peter Ho, Interview 4/24/2013, Melbourne, Australia

RAMÓN FERNÁNDEZ-ALONSO ARQUITECT www.fernandezalonso.com
Ramón Fernández-Alonso, Interview 10/28/2013, Granada, Spain

SCHEMATA ARCHITECTURE www.schemata.jp
Jo Nagasaka, Interview 05/07/2013, Tokyo, Japan

SEAN GODSELL ARCHITECTS www.seangodsell.com
Sean Godsell, Interview 04/22/2013, Melbourne, Australia

STUDIO505 www.studio505.com.au
Dylan Brady and Dirk Zimmermann, Interview 04/22/2013, Melbourne, Australia

TNA ARCHITECTS ww.tna-arch.com

UNEMORI ARCHITECTS www.unemori-archi.com
Hiroyuki Unemori, Interview 05/02/2013, Tokyo, Japan

VOLUAR ARQUITECTURA www.voluar.com,
Borja Lomas, Interview 10/25/2013, Madrid, Spain

ABOUT THE AUTHOR

Born and raised in Oakland, California, Andrew Michler, LEED AP BD+C, CPHC, found his way to a pine forest in the Colorado Rockies where he has lived off-grid since 1995. Merging work in design/construction, visual arts, and sustainable building research he has written extensively about sustainability in architecture.

His research has also led him to investigate Passive House. He designed and built the first international certified Passive House in Colorado which is free of foam and other toxic materials. Michler consults, through his firm Baosol llc, on low impact and adaptive building design and materials.

His wide-ranging exploration of design and environmental impact has led him all over the world. Exploring the edges of contemporary environmental architecture has helped Michler come to terms with the complex relationship between our built and natural environments.

More about his work www.baosol.com

twitter @andrewmichler